Exploring Experiences of Advocacy
by People with Learning Disabilities

of related interest

Deinstitutionalization and People with Intellectual Disabilities
In and Out of Institutions
Edited by Kelley Johnson and Rannveig Traustadóttir
ISBN 1 84310 101 7

Women With Intellectual Disabilities
Finding a Place in the World
Edited by Rannveig Traustadóttir and Kelley Johnson
ISBN 1 85302 846 0

Advocacy and Learning Disability
Edited by Barry Gray and Robin Jackson
ISBN 1 85302 942 4

Working with People with Learning Disabilities
Theory and Practice
David Thomas and Honor Woods
ISBN 1 85302 973 4

Person Centred Planning and Care Management with People
with Learning Disabilities
Edited by Paul Cambridge and Steven Carnaby
ISBN 1 84310 131 9

Helping People with a Learning Disability Explore Choice
Eve and Neil Jackson
Illustrated by Tim Baker
ISBN 1 85302 694 8

Inclusive Research with People with Learning Disabilities
Past, Present and Futures
Jan Walmsley and Kelley Johnson
ISBN 1 84310 061 pb

Quality of Life and Disability
An Approach for Community Practitioners
Ivan Brown and Roy I. Brown
Foreword by Ann and Rud Turnbull
ISBN 1 84310 005 3

Guide to Mental Health for Families and Carers of People
with Intellectual Disabilities
Geraldin Holt, Anastasis Gratsa, Nick Bouras, Teresa Joyce, Mary Jane Spiller
and Steve Hardy
ISBN 1 84310 277 3

Exploring Experiences of Advocacy by People with Learning Disabilities

Testimonies of Resistance

Edited by Duncan Mitchell,
Rannveig Traustadóttir, Rohhss Chapman,
Louise Townson, Nigel Ingham and Sue Ledger

Jessica Kingsley Publishers
London and Philadelphia

The eulogy for Roy Loomis by Shirley Dean in Chapter 2 is reproduced by permission of Shirley Dean.

First published in 2006
by Jessica Kingsley Publishers
116 Pentonville Road
London N1 9JB, UK
and
400 Market Street, Suite 400
Philadelphia, PA 19106, USA

www.jkp.com

Library of Congress Cataloging in Publication Data
A CIP catalog record for this book is available from the Library of Congress

British Library Cataloguing in Publication Data
A CIP catalogue record for this book is available from the British Library

ISBN-13: 978 1 84310 359 2
ISBN-10: 1 84310 359 1

Printed and bound in Great Britain by
Athenaeum Press, Gateshead, Tyne and Wear

Contents

1

Introduction

Duncan Mitchell

This book explores ways in which people with learning difficulties have spoken for themselves and resisted oppression. By adopting an approach that combines the accounts of people with learning disabilities, workers in learning disability services and academics, the editors hope to promote debate about the way in which different stakeholders in services relate to each other. Most of the chapters are drawn from experiences in the UK but accounts from Australia, Canada, Iceland and the USA broaden the book's perspective, giving it an international flavour.

'Testimonies of resistance' forms the theme of the book. This is partly due to the nature of the stories, which give examples of struggle against prevailing ideas and practices. It is also a clear attempt to highlight the work necessary if people with learning disabilities are to continue to develop ways of directing their own lives and playing a full part in their communities. The editors also wanted to encourage the contributors to consider the positive part they have played in changing services. They present to the reader an active and assertive group of people that counters the passive image of people with learning disabilities that is so often portrayed.

As a series of personal accounts combined with some academic reflection on the subject of learning disabilities, the book adds to the literature of life history, biography and experience of learning difficulty. In it, a period of contemporary history is charted in which people with learning difficulties have increasingly begun to speak for themselves. The contribution of families, carers and professionals in supporting change is also recognized, as is the fact that, while many oppressed groups have spoken for themselves for many years and hence been able to influence others and shape policy, people with learning difficulties have had less opportunity to do this.

The origins of this book are in the work of the Social History of Learning Disability Group based at the Open University. This group brings together academics, people with learning disabilities, service providers and other interested people to explore the past and its influence on the present and future. The group has addressed key issues in the history of learning disabilities and has been widely acclaimed for its approach of working with people with learning disabilities and integrating the stories of different individuals with varying backgrounds. The group's conferences have provided a forum in which the editors have met to draw together their work. Unsurprisingly given the emphasis of the conferences most of the published work has explicitly been related to the history of learning disability. However, some of the papers presented at the conferences have taken a more contemporary approach to the subject. This is likely to have been for two reasons. In the first place, when people are encouraged to tell their life stories it is inevitable that some will address a very recent period. This is not only the case with people in their twenties and thirties but also much older people who have preferred to reflect on the last ten years of their life rather than their experience of previous decades. Second, as the conferences have developed they have naturally moved towards covering different areas and while some of the themes have been similar there has been less emphasis on the experience of large institutions and far more on life within ordinary communities.

A number of the papers presented at their conferences form the basis of this book. The authors seek to address the key issues of advocacy and self-advocacy in contemporary services by presenting personal stories of the way in which people with learning disabilities and their supporters have resisted poor services, damaging attitudes and oppressive practice. Several issues have been raised in the conferences that are pertinent to current policy and practice in learning disability services. Prominent among these is the relationships between disabled and non-disabled people. There are examples of complex negotiation between people with learning difficulties and staff paid to work with them, their families, friends and volunteer workers. Questions regarding the nature of employment and power are exposed within some stories as people have had to wrestle with dilemmas about whether to employ help, accept it from people already employed or from volunteers.

The four sections of this book start with the personal stories before moving to group accounts, then alliances with others and ending with a series of reflections and interpretations of resistance within learning disability services. Part I contains personal accounts of advocacy and resistance including a biography of Ray Loomis and Tom Houlihan, two pioneers of self-advocacy. The discussion by Gudrún Stefánsdóttir and Rannveig Traustadóttir in Chapter 7 of the experiences of women with learning disabilities in Iceland also provides an international flavour. In Chapter 8 Sue Ledger and Lindy Shufflebotham examine a selection of songs of resistance from a number of institutions for people with learning disabilities in the UK; these demonstrate both resistance and the resilience of people living in long-stay institutions and the authors suggest links between the resistance of people with learning disabilities and that of other social groups.

Part II, 'Speaking for Ourselves: Accounts of Self-advocacy in Action', contains three chapters that reflect on the way that self-advocacy is developing by giving specific accounts of self-advocacy in action. Starting with the account by Paul Savage, Tina Wilkinson and Carl Worth of the way in which the Sheffield Speaking Up For Action Group (SUFA) began and developed from an initial idea to becoming a mature organization employing its own development worker, Part II contains accounts of several different self-advocacy organizations. Representing areas within England as far apart as Carlisle and Southend, the accounts present a picture of both similarities and differences of self-advocacy in action.

Part III, 'Alliances with Others', contains six accounts. Jessa Chupik describes a parents' group that grew from a small group of parents in Toronto to one of the largest and influential learning disability pressure groups in Canada. Elizabeth Tilley analyses the role of resistance within Mencap (a large British interest group), as well as the external activities of the group itself. Chapters 14 and 15 are biographies of people who have worked in the field of learning disabilities, and finally, Kelley Johnson offers observations on the way in which some women in Australia have taken a stand against the systems that have tried to manage their lives.

Part IV takes a more reflective view of advocacy and is designed to provoke thought about different ways of looking at the subject. Pamela Dale re-examines caring strategies of the past by considering how people have been able to live within oppressive systems by conforming or resisting. Melanie Nind asks whether people with profound learning difficulties use behaviours that are often seen as meaningless or harmful to gain some control and to resist unwelcome demands and situations.

The use of language has been, and remains, hugely important to people with learning disabilities and is an ongoing political issue. Terms such as 'mental deficiency', 'subnormality' and 'mental handicap' have been used widely in the past. Language not only describes contemporary views and concepts of difference but also contributes to its development. The dilemma for those of us writing about the past is whether to use language from the period being discussed or whether to adopt current terminology to avoid offence and to help foster a positive image of people with learning disabilities. The compromise is generally to avoid confusion by using language from the past in direct quotations, and when absolutely necessary for clarity, and to use modern language at all other times. This guide does not help with the current debate about whether to use the term 'learning difficulty', a term that is preferred by many people with learning difficulties in the UK, or 'learning disability' which has become the preferred term of the UK Government and is widely used within services. The editors have avoided having to choose between these options by leaving it to the authors of each chapter to decide. As a result both terms appear in this volume. International comparisons further confuse the use of terminology and it may therefore be helpful to point out that the use of the terms 'learning difficulties' and 'learning disabilities' in the UK is similar to the use of 'intellectual disabilities' and 'developmental disabilities' in other countries.

Many people who have been labelled as having learning disabilities have not been able to lead ordinary lives. This is because of the views of people who have had the power to determine where people with learning disabilities live. Many people with learning disabilities have resisted the views of others by struggling to lead ordinary lives. One such person is Mary Coventry, who testified to her own resistance at a conference at the Open University in 2001 and wanted her story to be included in this book.

> I would like to talk about my work, hobbies and interests and my various achievements. I feel that I have worked hard and achieved a lot in the last few years. I lived at home with my family first of all, but now I live more or less independently in a group home. I work at the People First office in Croydon once a fortnight on Tuesdays, and I go to Mencap meetings in London with People First. I enjoy writing poetry, and my other hobbies and interests are varied. They are knitting, crochet, tapestry, embroidery and collecting models and pictures of owls. I am interested in oasthouses, windmills and watermills and I am knowledgeable about things like flowers and plants and the different species of owls. I have been on lots of different college courses over the years. These include maths and English. I have lots of friends and a boyfriend called John.

Mary wanted this story to stand as it is, without expansion or further detail. For Mary, as with many other people, this account illustrates the power of the ordinary. Ironically the fight to live ordinary lives has led to a number of quite extraordinary life stories, some of which are discussed in the pages that follow.

PART I

Personal Accounts of Advocacy and Resistance

2

Advocacy as Resistance
Speaking Up as a Way of Fighting Back

Dorothy Atkinson, Mabel Cooper and Gloria Ferris

Gloria Ferris and Mabel Cooper lived in a long-stay hospital for many years. They write about how they became involved in speaking up for others. Gloria worked with a young woman who also lived in the hospital and could not speak for herself. When they left the hospital Gloria continued to visit her and has now become her advocate. Gloria talks about how she was an advocate before she knew about the word. Mabel tells us about how she did not talk very much for a long time. This changed after she got involved with People First in Croydon and began to talk a great deal. She became Chairperson of Croydon People First and London People First. After she gave up being Chairperson she carried on speaking on the radio and writing for *Community Care*.

Introduction
'Advocacy' means speaking up for yourself or others. The history of self-advocacy, as we understand it now, is of relatively recent origin in the UK. It

started in a small way in the 1970s, taking off properly in 1984 with the formation of People First, London. Yet people with learning difficulties were 'speaking out' in one way or another long before that, long before the terms 'advocacy' and 'self-advocacy' came into vogue.

In this chapter, Mabel Cooper and Gloria Ferris give their first-hand accounts of what it was like to speak up in the past and what it is like to do so nowadays. The term 'advocacy' was not used in the 1950s when these stories began, but did exist. It often took the form of resistance, especially in the long-stay hospitals. This was the origin of both advocacy (speaking up for others) and self-advocacy (speaking up for yourself). Some of the people who spoke up for others years ago went on to become advocates: this was the experience of Gloria Ferris, as she explains in her story. Other people went on to form the self-advocacy groups and the People First organizations of the 1980s, 1990s and the present. Mabel Cooper describes how she got involved in the self-advocacy movement in later years, after she left St Lawrence's Hospital in Caterham, Surrey.

The three of us have worked together on many occasions, including our early work on co-researching and writing life stories. The format we devised then still serves us well. This involves tape-recorded conversations around themes – in this instance advocacy and resistance – which I (Dorothy Atkinson) transcribe and put into a 'story' format. We then read this together and make whatever changes are needed. The two stories below were produced in this way and are the final approved versions. They are entirely in the words of the two authors (Mabel Cooper and Gloria Ferris), though I had a hand in putting them together.

Speaking Up for Muriel *by Gloria Ferris*

How it all began

I've known Muriel for over 45 years, since 1956, when we were both in St Lawrence's Hospital in Caterham, Surrey. Of course, she was quite young when I took her on, nine or ten, I can't remember just what age she was. Her parents have both passed on; she's got a brother but they don't keep in touch. I'm her lifeline, and she's mine, more or less, although I've got other relatives. They know that I go to see her and I look after her, I do things for her.

I met Muriel in St Lawrence's when she was very young. She was on C1 and I met her there when I took over and helped the staff out. Muriel's family came from Shepherd's Bush. I think her father owned a café or shop there. They were good parents; they never missed a week without going to see her. Twice a week they'd come, even when they retired to Brighton. They never missed. They were good people, they never complained. Her parents were very good to me. We used to go out together because they couldn't lift Muriel, they couldn't manage her. We used to have tea in the pavilion in the hospital grounds.

I helped the staff out on C1. They [the residents] quite enjoyed it because it helped them out. I dressed them, put them in nightdresses; I was a good help to them. I quite enjoyed being with them, especially Muriel. She is a happy sort of person. She's got a lovely smile. When you take pictures, sometimes she's not in the mood for people taking pictures of her – and she won't smile, won't even look at you. She'll look the other way. I'd never forget her. I told her parents that if anything happened to them I would never forget her. And now I'm registered as an advocate for her, so I'm near enough the next of kin.

When I first went to St Lawrence's I went to the admissions ward; later I went to B3. It was what they called a 'high grade' ward. There was people going out to daily jobs or to work on different wards, or the laundry or wherever. I mostly went down to C1, which I quite enjoyed doing. C1 was for people with severe disabilities, people in wheelchairs, and with cerebral palsy and other things. Muriel was transferred to C1 because of being in a wheelchair. I dealt with Muriel specially. I thought she was the person I rather enjoyed being with. I washed Muriel, dressed her, cleaned her teeth, did all those sort of things. I really did enjoy being with her, and a lot of other people who were there. I worked with the nurses. Although I wasn't a nurse, I helped them out and I quite enjoyed it. I made beds, I was in the bathroom, and I was dressing them, doing their hair, and then sometimes putting them to bed, which I quite enjoyed. I loved it.

I was in my early thirties when I left St Lawrence's. I visited Muriel every week for the next 20 or so years while I was working at different places in Croydon. Then in 1994 I got made redundant. That's when I became an advocate for Muriel. And that was the year she left St Lawrence's and went to Whitehill House to live. It's a home for 12 clients. It's quite a nice house and they've got a big kitchen.

I go to see Muriel two days a week, Wednesdays and Thursdays. When I first arrive her face lights up! She's really quite happy. I spend the whole day there; I leave there at seven o'clock at night. I get there about ten or half past ten. Muriel can't feed herself at all. So when I get up there I feed her, wash her, bath her, do her hair, put some cream on her face. I do everything for her! And I put her to bed. I'd like to visit Muriel more than only two days a week. It would be nice to see her every day, but it's difficult getting there.

It's what I really like doing, I like being with Muriel and people like her. It's what I am. I like to help, and I like to mix with other people. I'm part of Muriel's family now. I always thought she was special. She looks forward to it too, and I think she must miss it when I'm not there. If you've got a tongue in your head to speak for yourself then you speak up. Like Muriel, she can't speak, so I speak for her and ask for the things that she needs done for her. That's what they call 'being an advocate'. Doing the things that she needs and what she wants. I love it. I love life as it is now.

How Advocacy Partners got started

Nowadays I'm called an advocate, though I'm still doing all the things with Muriel that I've been doing for 45 years. I was doing it before it got a name and became part of government policy. I'm an advocate for an organization called 'Advocacy Partners'. It wasn't always called that. It was called 'Advocacy Alliance' when it first started. But I didn't know about it then. At the time Advocacy Alliance was starting up I was speaking up for Muriel and supporting her in St Lawrence's (as I had been doing for over 30 years by then).

Advocacy Alliance was started in 1981, when five charities got together to launch what's called 'citizen advocacy'. The charities were Mind, the Spastics Society (now called Scope), Mencap, One-to-One and the Leonard Cheshire Foundation. They set up a new organization called Advocacy Alliance. The idea in those days was to find advocates for people living in St Lawrence's as well as in two other long-stay hospitals. The other two were St Ebba's in Epsom and Normansfield in Teddington.

In 1987, Advocacy Alliance split into two separate organizations. One was called 'Citizen Advocacy Alliance'. This carried on the work in the three hospitals. Although I had left St Lawrence's by then, I was still visiting Muriel. I was there every week, but never came across Citizen Advocacy Alliance. Their job was to find advocates for people who had no visiting relatives or friends from outside. As Muriel had me to visit she probably didn't qualify for help. At that time there were 45,000 people living in long-stay hospitals around the country, many of them never receiving a visitor from one year to the next.

As people began to leave the long-stay hospitals, including St Lawrence's, advocates were found to work with people who were moving into the community. Also advocates were found for people who were already living in the community. Citizen Advocacy Alliance grew a lot during the 1980s and 1990s. They got funding to take on more staff, and recruited more and more volunteers to become advocates. I became a registered advocate with them in 1994. In 1996 the name changed to Advocacy Partners, which is what it is today. As well as being Muriel's advocate, I'm also on the management committee.

I enjoy being an advocate, but I've also got a lot out of it. It's given me confidence to speak up for myself. I've got involved in lots of different things like writing my life story and giving talks at conferences. I'm on the Partnership Board for Croydon learning disabilities and I help with person-centred planning. I think that through being an advocate for Muriel all those years, I've also become a self-advocate, able to speak up for myself. Now Mabel will talk about the history of self-advocacy.

From Saying Nothing to Speaking Up *by Mabel Cooper*
How I got started

I was in St Lawrence's Hospital for over 20 years. There was nothing when we came out of hospital. No support, no help. There's more help now but there wasn't anything when I first came out.

Nowadays I can speak up for myself but I didn't when I first came out. When I was in St Lawrence's I didn't hardly speak at all. I only said 'yes' or 'no' and mostly I only said 'no'. I didn't say many words at all when I first came out of St Lawrence's. No wonder. I wasn't quite sure whether I'd get into trouble, that sort of thing. When I went to live at Isabel's place she says to me, 'Are you going to join People First? So you'll talk more than you do otherwise you just say "yes" or "no" or nod your head.' So I said, 'Oh, all right, I'll go and see what it's like.' So down I go to Croydon People First.

It was Kathy who started it. She went to college and heard about People First so she set it up. She wrote around to see how many people could join in Croydon. We used to go to Bramley Hill and meet there in the office. Then they moved office to Blake Hall in Borough Road. Then they moved to Katherine Street where they are now. There were about ten people when I first joined, more men than women.

When I first went up to Bramley Hill I sat and listened. That's all, I sat and listened. I did that for a month. I joined People First and they didn't tell you to shut up, so I kept on going. I said a few words but not enough to be able to do the things I do now. I think being in a group teaches you that you've got to learn to say what you want to say and not what everybody else wants you to say.

After about a month, Kathy said to me, 'We're going to have an AGM. Would you do the Chair?' So I did the Chairing for Croydon People First and then Mary Coventry joined up. I said, 'Well let Mary be my secretary because she can read.' So Mary got to be my secretary. I did Croydon People First for four years in the Chair, and then I did London for six years as chairperson and vice-chairperson.

Then we went up to London because they had their AGM. I went up to London and put my name in for being the Chair in London. People First in London started before Croydon; it was the first in the country. It got started after a group of people went to America in 1984. A lady called Alison went, and they set it up when they got back. They had a little office first then they moved to King's Cross. In London they did voting at their meetings and you couldn't stay in the room if you wanted to stand for being chairperson. I thought I'd stand and see what happens. I had to say my name and who I was, and then we went out. Kelley (who is now my friend) said, 'You've all got to come back.' And she whispered in my ear, 'You're the Chair!' So I knew already when they called us back in and told us. I got the most votes and became the chairperson. Then they had another lot of voting for vice-chairperson.

So afterwards when they told me, I said 'OK' and I said to Kelley, 'Can I have a word with you?' I said, 'What do I have to do for the Chair because I don't read that well. I would find it difficult.' She said, 'Do nothing – we'll help you.' So I was Chair of London and Chair of Croydon at that time. I did both, Croydon and London. And then, because Declan was there then, Declan used to say, 'Come in on Mondays and help us make tea. We'll teach you to use the computer and you can go out speaking to people and that will help you with your speaking problem.' So that's how it started, and ever since then People First has been my lifeline, other than Mencap. People First did me well really. It was the first organization I joined after I came out of St Lawrence's.

Being Chair of London People First

As Chair of London People First I did all sorts of things. I had to go to different places and meet new people in each one. We went to schools, day centres and hospitals visiting people, supporting other groups. I was still Chair of Croydon People First, because at that time I was Chair of both Croydon and London. Then I said to Kathy, 'I'm not going to put myself forward for the next one, for the simple reason that I'm doing London. I'm bringing reports back from London to Croydon People First. I don't want to keep on doing both.'

So I gave up the Croydon one, the Chair that is, not altogether. I'm still a member and I'm still on their committee, and I help them in every way I can. I still go to the office – it's now in Katherine Street. Mary helps me write letters and we do other bits of work, but I don't always go to their meetings. I still belong to People First but I do a lot of other things now – I speak on the radio, I do interviews, I go to conferences and I write for *Community Care*.

That all started when I was still Chair of London People First. I don't do London any more either. London finished. But while I was there, I used to go out a lot, talking to people. One of the places we went to was a group in Teddington. They were people who still lived in Normansfield Hospital. I went there, and Dorothy came to see if they would like to tell their life stories. None of them would do it because they were frightened of the staff. In the end we had to let the staff in and they were frightened and none of them would do it. So, on the train home I said to Dorothy, 'I'd love to be able to do that, to tell my life story – especially about St Lawrence's.'

So that's how all this started. We worked together on my life story and it came out in a book called *Forgotten Lives* (Atkinson, Jackson and Walmsley 1997). Since then I've been asked to talk to all sorts of people about my life, and the lives of other people with learning difficulties. I'm still speaking up, but I'm doing it in a different way – through books, radio, TV and conferences. I'm not just speaking up for myself, I'm speaking up for other people with learning difficulties so that everyone knows what life was like for us then and what it's like for us today. I'm supporting other people to tell their stories; it's letting the world know what it's like now and what it was like then. It's still advocacy but it's doing it in a different way.

Conclusion

The lives of Mabel Cooper and Gloria Ferris are very different today to how they were 50 years ago when they were long-stay residents in St Lawrence's Hospital. And yet, their resistance then to their allotted roles and people's low expectations of them became part of what has turned out to be a longer story of the emergence of advocacy and self-advocacy. They spoke up when speaking up had no name. Now they are part of a national and international advocacy and self-advocacy movement.

But that is only part of what they do. In the roles, relationships and responsibilities that they have taken on in their lives in the community, they continue to resist the labels that other people have long sought to give them. They are part of a continuing story of resistance by people with learning difficulties.

Reference

Atkinson, D., Jackson, M. and Walmsley, J. (eds) (1997) *Forgotten Lives: Exploring the History of Learning Disability.* Kidderminster: BILD Publishers.

3

Restriction and Resistance

The Experience of Life on a Locked Ward
for People with Learning Disabilities

Katherine Owen

Katherine Owen spent a lot of time with 11 women who lived in hospital on a locked ward. She got to know them well and wants to tell us about their life in the hospital. She describes how the women had to live with a lot of rules but also how they had ways of fighting the rules. The women found ways to get what they wanted and were also able to show themselves to be individuals by resisting the hospital rules and routines.

Introduction

In this chapter, I will describe various strategies of resistance used by women with severe learning disabilities who lived on a locked ward of an old long-stay hospital. Although government policy has been committed to the closure of old long-stay hospitals for over 50 years, in 2001 some 1500 men and women still remained living on wards in long-stay hospitals (Department of Health 2001). The observations on which this chapter is based were carried out as part of an ethnographic study that took place between 1999 and 2002. Here, I will briefly outline the study and then describe some of the ways in which the women resisted both the system in which they lived and the labels and stereotypes by which they were known. I will demonstrate that they fought hard on a daily basis to express themselves, assert themselves and get their individual needs met. In this way I argue against Goffman's assertion that inmates living in institutions necessarily experience the 'mortification process', which involves a 'curtailment of the self' and a giving up of individual will (Goffman 1961, p.48).

The study

The study, based at St George's Hospital Medical School and funded by The Judith Trust, aimed to explore how women with severe learning disabilities experienced moving from a locked ward of an old long-stay hospital into homes in the community. A more detailed description of the research can be found in *'Going Home?' A Study of Women with Severe Learning Disabilities Moving Out of a Locked Ward* (Owen 2004). There were 11 women in the study. All were described as having learning disabilities and challenging behaviour. Most were described as having severe learning disabilities and some had additional mental health problems. They were aged between 28 and 72, and the majority had lived in long-stay hospital provision since early childhood. The data were collected predominantly using methods of participant observation. This involved spending many hours with the women, at all times of the day and night, for more than 18 months, first on the locked ward and then in their new homes. In this chapter, only the data collected from the time spent with them on the locked ward are used. On the ward I spent many hours sitting beside the women on the sofas in their day-room, being with them as they ate their meals, helping them to dress or change into clean clothes, and going for walks with them around the hospital grounds or to sessions at their day centre. I wanted to get to know them, get to know what was important to them and the rhythm of their daily lives.

Restriction

The features of institutional life have been well documented over the years, for example by Goffman (1961), Oswin (1971) and Ryan and Thomas (1987). Goffman famously described features of the 'total institution' as he saw them. These included the fact that all aspects of life are conducted in the same place, all the day's activities are tightly scheduled and activities are carried out with large numbers of others, all doing the same thing at the same time. Many features of life on the locked ward fitted the description of a total institution made by Goffman.

The hospital was literally the whole world that the women knew. For the majority, their lives were lived out within a 500-yard radius and for the most part they were cut off from wider society. Their daily activities were carried out in the company of others, largely doing the same thing at the same time. One of the most striking examples was bath times. This involved one member of staff being in the bathroom and bathing all the women who wanted a bath, one member of staff being in the shower-room and showering all those who wanted a shower, and other members of staff taking dirty sheets off the beds and putting out the women's clothes for the day. The women waited for their turn in the corridors.

Life on the ward also featured various schedules and rules that the women lived by. For example, they could only have a cup of tea after meals and at 11 am and 4 pm, and could only have a bath in the morning or evening unless they were particularly 'soiled' or were considered 'high' (this was the way that the staff described women who showed signs of being excited or too loud). There were rules about where they could go, both inside and outside the ward, rules about behaviour and even rules about the expression of emotion. For example, the locking of doors ensured the women were limited in where they could go. All the rooms were locked apart from the toilets and an area of compartmentalized bed space shared by four of the women. The staff alone held keys and the women therefore had to ask permission if they wanted to go elsewhere. Rules about behaviour were particularly strict at mealtimes. The women were often told to 'Sit down', 'Sit up straight' and 'Be quiet'. The rules surrounding emotions meant that when the women cried or showed sadness or distress they were often removed from the day-room or told to 'Give us a smile' or 'Say you're happy'.

Resisting rules

The women had various ways in which they asserted their wishes, preferences and desires in the face of the restrictive nature of the ward. At mealtimes, one of the women would get around being made to eat by either being sick in the toilet after a meal or dropping her food onto the floor so it would be too dirty to eat. Others would push their food carefully on to the plates of others. One of the women would avoid being moved back to her seat, if she had got up, by sitting down on the floor. In terms of structures, those who were verbal would ask for cups of tea or baths outside of the allotted times. They would be told, 'It's not time yet', but still, day after day, they would ask. The women who were non-verbal asserted themselves in different ways. Two of the women would wait by the kitchen door, in case there was a moment when they could get an 'extra' cup of tea. One of the women, Francesca, would take people by the hand to show them where she wanted to go and what she wanted to do.

In the early days of my time on the ward, Francesca tried several times to get me to help her change into pyjamas on her return from the day service. The rules of the ward did not allow this. She knew that I sometimes had a key and that I was naïve about ward rules, and used these facts to her advantage.

If I was sitting down in the day-room, she would come and sit next to me. She would start by uncrossing my legs, carefully but firmly, and then pull me to my feet. She would then take my hand and lead me to the bathroom door. Once unlocked, she would immediately undress and sit on the toilet. When she had finished, she would carefully choose the pair of pyjamas she wanted to wear, from the pile on the bathroom cabinet. It was important to Francesca that the top and bottom of the pyjamas matched. If there was not a matching pair in the bathroom, she would lead me to her bedroom, and then to her wardrobe, so that again I could unlock the doors, and finally she would be able to find the pink top that would go with her pink bottoms.

If staff ignored her requests, Francesca would get frustrated. She would drag staff members off chairs and across rooms, trying to get them to where she wanted to go. She would deliberately urinate so that staff would have to take her to change her clothes. Finally, she would hit herself, or use someone else's hand to hit herself, usually against the mouth.

This account shows that Francesca was not passive to the dictates of the ward, but that she would put all her energy into getting her needs met. It shows that she cleverly used her knowledge of the system and the staff to identify weaknesses, for example approaching new people who would not know the rules of the ward so well. It also shows that she used various strategies to get what she wanted, from uncrossing people's legs and pulling them to their feet, to leading them where she wanted to go, to undressing herself. Finally, it shows that Francesca would be forced to go to extreme measures, urinating on her clothes or hitting herself or others, in order to get herself heard. This story is important because it highlights that, after 40 years of institutional living, Francesca was still prepared to fight for who she was and what she wanted, and give her life meaning.

Resisting labels

The women had various ways in which they would resist the labels and stereo-types by which they were known. A good example of this is how the women moved beyond being known as genderless, non-sexual children. On the ward it could be seen that the women were treated like children by the language that was used to describe them. They were collectively known as 'the girls'. Their day service was referred to as 'school'. They were 'told off' for 'playing up' or for being 'naughty'. The exclusion of the women from the category of adult woman has been explained as coming from the deep need of the staff to separate themselves from the people they cared for (Menzies Lyth 1990).

However, the women clearly asserted their femininity, their womanhood and their sexuality. They asserted their femininity by attending to their appearance. They would make it clear when they wanted to wear smart clothes, clothes that coordinated (as seen in the previous example of Francesca), that made them feel good, were clean and without holes or missing buttons. Some of the women would make it known they wanted to wear make-up. I would be led to make-up boxes on the tops of wardrobes, or have conversations about 'eyes' with their fingers stroking their lids showing how they wanted brushes to apply eye-shadow. Other women would repeatedly say when they wanted their hair cut. This involved a hairdresser coming to the ward and cutting all the women's hair on the same morning, and more or less always in the same short style. Other women, who had had extensive teeth extractions, would often use their fingers or their tongue to go to the places in their mouths where their teeth used to be. Alternatively, one of the women often talked about 'dentists' and asked repeatedly when her next appointment would be.

The women asserted their womanhood in several ways. One of the main ways was by asserting their position within acknowledged gendered roles – as daughters, sisters, mothers, partners and lovers. One of the women, who lived on the ward, was a mother. She had given birth to her daughter after a relationship with a soldier. Shortly afterwards, the child had been given up for adoption. Over 50 years later, Elizabeth spent her time on the ward carrying a bear that she called 'Jimmy'. She related to the bear as if it were her child. At different times I saw her cradle it in her arms, sing to it, lift her top up to breast-feed it, carefully stroke the hair away from its eyes and even give it sips of her tea before she would drink it herself. In this way, it can be seen how Elizabeth lived out the role of motherhood on a daily basis.

One of the most powerful ways in which the women resisted the assumptions that they were not sexual beings was through asserting their sexuality. Some of the more verbal women would talk frequently about men, wanting a man or directly wanting sex. One of the women was particularly fascinated by the male staff, and male visitors to the ward. She would become excited, laugh loudly, talk quickly and try and engage them in conversation. She would say several times a day, 'I want a man.' Another woman was similarly preoccupied by men, but would be more sexually explicit. She would talk about 'cocks', invite me and members of staff to come and have a bath with her, or to share her bed. Other women, who were non-verbal, would take every opportunity to leave the ward, thus increasing the chances they had to meet men.

It can thus be seen that in this restrictive environment the women did what they could to resist the stereotypical ways in which they were known by others and assert their wills and their identity, as feminine, sensual, sexual, thinking, feeling, experiencing women.

Conclusion

From the descriptions given, it can be seen that the concept of resistance is not straightforward. The strategies worked to varying degrees of success in getting the women's needs met or in altering how others saw them. There were both compromises and dilemmas that the women faced. The women were often left with no option but to comply with the various demands and wishes of the staff. Moreover, there was often a cost to be borne for asserting themselves. In the case of Francesca, the extreme measures she went to involved compromising different parts of herself. Other costs included 'getting into trouble' with the staff and consequently having privileges or other things that were of importance to individuals withdrawn, for example leaving the ward, having cigarettes or getting access to bedrooms.

However, such accounts of resistance are important. They add to what is known about people with severe learning disabilities, they legitimize their experiences and they challenge assumptions that are made about them, for example that they are passive victims of oppressive service systems, incapable and dependent. It is thus vital to acknowledge that in spite of the depersonalizing effects of institutional life, described so vividly by Goffman (1961), people with severe learning disabilities can continue to maintain their selves, their uniqueness and their individual ways of being human.

References

Department of Health (2001) *Valuing People: A New Strategy for Learning Disability for the 21st Century.* London: The Stationery Office.

Goffman, E. (1961) *Asylums: Essays on the Social Situation of Mental Patients and Other Inmates.* London: Pelican.

Menzies Lyth, I. (1990) 'Social systems as a defence against anxiety: An empirical study of the nursing service of a general hospital', in E. Trist and H. Murray (eds) *The Social Engagement of Social Science, vol. 1, The Social-Psychological Perspective.* London: Free Association Books.

Oswin, M. (1971) *The Empty Hours: A Study of the Weekend Life of Handicapped Children in Institutions.* Harmondsworth: Penguin Books.

Owen, K. (2004) *'Going Home?' A Study of Women with Severe Learning Disabilities Moving Out of a Locked Ward.* London: The Judith Trust.

Ryan, J. and Thomas, F. (1987) *The Politics of Mental Handicap.* London: Free Association Books.

4

'I Would Never Walk, Talk, Sit or Stand!'

The Girl on the Tricycle

Marjorie Chappell with Duncan Mitchell

Marjorie Chappell now lives on her own and spends some of her time working on her computer and giving talks to groups of people about her life. She has written her life story and this chapter is a part of her story. She writes about how she has always struggled to lead an independent life. She has done this with the help of her mother and also with a great deal of effort by herself. Marjorie has cerebral palsy. She was born in 1929 when things were very different from the way they are now.

Introduction

Marjorie Chappell was born with cerebral palsy and she does not have learning disabilities. Her story features in this book because her life has been characterized by resistance to the view of some others that she would not achieve an independent life. Her testimony has been an inspiration to many, including people with learning disabilities, to whom she has related her story on an individual basis and at many meetings and conferences. She has fought against negative views all her life, whether they have been held by officials, acquaintances or members of her own family. Marjorie's story is both simple and complex. Simple, because it is a story about a family, the framework of which most people will recognize. Complex, because it is a story of resistance with and against some of the same people: Marjorie has often been in conflict with friends and family in order to be able to determine her own best interests.

Marjorie's story

The first example of resistance in my story is my survival itself. My parents had been married for over two years when I arrived in 1929. No-one ever wanted a daughter more than my father and mother. On 28 March, after a lot of struggling for hours I was eventually literally pulled through the bed rails of an iron bedstead and I was here. Mother did not know what was happening to her or me until the following day as she almost lost her life through my birth. I weighed in at 12 pounds and the doctor and nurse put me aside as dead as obviously I had not taken that vital first breath properly. My grandmother was there and, after the doctor had gone, she took my battered and blue body downstairs, warmed me up and dressed me; she realized that I was having difficulty breathing but did not worry. As we know now that when a baby doesn't take its first breath naturally it can cause untold damage for the rest of the child's life. The long-awaited daughter was here and my name was Marjorie Joan.

My father went off to the many pubs around the town and bragged about his big bouncing baby girl leaving his young innocent wife to suffer so much pain as the birth had taken almost 12 hours. (If she had been examined during her pregnancy and I had been born by caesarean none of this would have happened and there were suggestions later that I should have been born a month earlier but it seems that Mother never saw a doctor or nurse until they were called when her waters burst.) Mother was as innocent as a newborn baby as to the joys of birth or how it happened. Apparently, she met the doctor in the street and told him that she thought that she was expecting a baby. As a doctor had to be paid in those dark days and some would not call without payment, he said to her 'Call me when you need me' as he knew there was little money around.

When the doctor returned sometime later, he ran upstairs and down again, and said to Grandma, 'I think she [Mother] will be all right if she lives until the morning.' Then he said, 'Shall I take it away?' Grandma said, 'Take what away?' He said, 'The dead baby, you don't want that left here, do you?' Grandma was horrified, and said, 'She is asleep.' With that the doctor went, without saying another word.

Then came many years, when Mother took me around to many different hospitals and as many different specialists who all gave a different diagnosis, from rickets to mental troubles. She began to worry that I had something very rare, for there was never a name given it to it. No-one ever mentioned anything like 'spastic' [cerebral palsy] for that is what I am. Nor did she ever see another child like me in all those years when she took me from hospital to hospital.

For three years Mother walked to various hospitals, with no money for the fare on the buses that passed by every few minutes of her 20-mile each way walk, and with train journeys to other hospitals paid for with money that should have bought food for her. One particular day, while holding me under the heat-ray lamp at the hospital, she collapsed and fainted from starvation. The doctor asked when she had had her last meal and, when she said 'I can't remember', he gave her two shillings and sixpence (which would have bought a banquet in those days) to go and buy a dinner while a nurse looked after the baby. She ate all she could, but quickly lost it all again as her stomach could not take it.

The following week, eight doctors were waiting for her. They led her into a private room, sat her in front of them and told her that her baby, who was now about three, would never sit, stand, walk, talk, was blind, could not hear and was mental. Please note, she was always alone as Father never ever took me anywhere. Mother told them that I was trying with her help to do all this and she knew I could see and hear. She was told coolly but firmly that this was just her maternal love and imagination. They made out forms for her to sign to have me put in a home there and then. She was told to just forget that she had ever had me and to go away and have more children as it could never happen again. Mother grabbed me up into her arms, cried and ran all the way home.

By this time we had moved to a village called Ferndown in Dorset; I had been born in Wimborne. Father always had work, of the manual kind; he also had a clean home, bed and a hot meal ready and waiting for him when he returned from work and expected it, whatever happened. This particular day he wasn't indoors when Mother and I got home from the hospital. He was down the garden talking to the neighbours waiting for her to come home and cook his tea. He would not come when Mother called him to tell him this shattering news. Father's reaction was always the same from that day on; when told they wanted to put me away, he agreed. 'That is the best thing to do. Get rid of the little bugger,' he said.

I feel very sad for my Dad, even today, in that he could never accept me as the daughter that he had dreamed of. He would never let me get near enough to him to love him, would never go out with me or tell anyone that I even existed. Although Derek was born six years later, normal and healthy, there must have been some happiness for both of them, but my birth was the end of the marriage and family life they had dreamed of.

The tricycle and the power of independence

Soon after we moved to Ferndown, Mother bought me my first tricycle, which had a rounded back. This was her own idea and she sat me on it, tied my feet to the pedals and my hands into a glove-like shield on the handlebars. It had a furl on the back into which she could put the end of a walking stick and push me. It being a fixed wheel meant my legs had to work, going round and round with the pedals. Away we went and if I hadn't had that tricycle I believe that I would never have sat up properly or walked or done anything. I would have been the proverbial 'cabbage' that doctors said I was. I have always been truly grateful to her for this as I would never have gone to school, walked enough to be able to get on and off all the future tricycles that were to follow, gone in shops or walked around indoors and short distances outdoors.

Walking wrongly for many years was to cause me a lot of pain in my teens. It led to operations on my hips and eventually put me into a wheelchair for the rest of my life, not able to walk even one step. With hindsight I now think this could have been avoided had I not been quite so cruel on my hips by what we called 'sprawling around' walking. This wore out my hip joints with every step I took, until they were both egg shaped and I could go on no longer. I have seen the same thing happening to spastic children today. They are given walking frames and walking sticks to get them on their feet. Anything to get them to 'walk' when they never will walk properly and will end up like me now, having also to cope with the additional problems of old age. My advice to anyone coping with a spastic child is to find out what they can or cannot do and concentrate on that, especially their brain and hand control.

Today whole communities are asked to raise money to send these children to the Peto Institute in Hungary for specialized treatment and tell the child that when it comes home, he/she is going to be able to walk, talk and play like his or her siblings and friends at school. This annoys me when children have the intelligence to understand such a cruel promise; money and exercises are forced upon them but they are going to return home with the same disability that will be theirs for the rest of their lives. I have watched documentaries about this so-called 'wonder cure' but all I see is exactly the kind of help mother gave to me for many years when she always seemed to find a way around most things that my unsteady hands would not work with my brain until between us we found the answer. The only thing the Peto has that we didn't is brightly coloured walking frames and things like that. Otherwise what they have is basically the same as the things Mother made for me, by beating up furniture and putting wheels on it, to try and encourage me to stand and eventually take my own balance and 'walk'. Is this yet another money-making racket in this day and age? Whenever I read of these 'instant cures', how I would love to intervene and tell the parent and everyone involved and tell them my story or rather my devoted mother's story.

The battle for education

After the usual long wait in a very damp and cold hall with one small finger of flame in a so-called gas fire, we finally got in to see this lady orthopaedic special-ist. I can see her now; she had known me a long time. All she ever did was to examine me, twisting my arms and legs and telling me to relax something with a very long name. Neither of us ever knew what she meant and I do not know to this day what it was that I was supposed to relax. However, after this ritual, Mother tentatively asked her, 'Can she go to school?' I could read, spell and write and all my little friends were at school, I knew where they were and I wanted to be with them. The first reaction was, 'How would she get to school?' Mother said, 'On her tricycle.' This the lady orthopaedic specialist would not believe, until they got me dressed and she saw me on my tricycle. This really amazed her, and not long after she had other disabled children up on tricycles, but still the word 'spastic' was never uttered by anyone.

Now on what I expect was the next day, Mother took me up to the village school, a council school, right at the top of a long steep hill. In those dark ages, there were no special schools but a few institution schools, where remember I would have probably been put with mentally handicapped children years before, had the medics had their way. Going to this council school was entirely up to the headmaster and the teacher. Having got there on my tricycle, I would need help to get to my desk and the toilet and if I stayed to dinner would need to be fed and washed afterwards. This was tried for half days for a few weeks, but I remember it wasn't very long before I was going every day, and woe betide anyone who tried to keep me away from my beloved school. School days were some of the happiest days of my life and the older I get the more grateful I am to all those teachers who helped me through those years. I feel that although I was the only disabled child in the school, I was treated the same as everyone else, just one of the girls. There was never anything 'special' about me as the school friends I still meet at our annual school reunion will tell anyone, we are all in our mid-seventies now. All I remember is that they were always ready to help me but only when necessary and, as they say, 'I was just one of the girls', the only difference being that they mostly walked to school in all winds and weather while I went everywhere with them on my tricycle.

A struggle for training

When it came time for me to leave school I was very reluctant but I had a chance to go to a rehabilitation college for disabled trainees at Exeter. So away I went. Mother took me there by train and had to leave me there for the first time in my life. I was not yet 15 years old and had left home with a suitcase and a tricycle. Life had really begun.

But then, before I knew it, I was shown how to make woolly balls on two rings of cardboard. This I had been doing all my life at home, along with embroidering little messages to my grandmothers and weaving on pieces of cardboard and trying to knit: no matter how many times the stitches came off, I did it in the end. Mother through the years had done everything she could to help me steady my hands. But 'woolly balls', when I had been told I was going away to be trained!

The next day I asked if I could use a typewriter and although the instructor said 'Yes' when I said that I wanted to train to be a typist she laughed at me and told me to go and sew woollen balls together. I managed to type a letter to Mum and the following weekend she arrived, by train and bus, with a great big heavy German-made typewriter. She must have gone to work extra hours or made a dozen dresses to get the money to buy this. So having done nothing else but type all day Sunday, I must have got someone to take it to the work-room on Monday morning to present it to the instructor who by now I regarded as 'The Dragon'. I can still hear her sneering at me. 'You will never be a typist,' she said, 'but you can play with it in your spare time, but not in here. We have decided to put you in the dressmakers' workshop.' 'If I could have been a dressmaker,' I told her, 'I would not be here', for Mother was a very good dressmaker whom I had watched and tried to copy all my life.

After being at the college for about a month and getting nowhere fast I was introduced to weaving by an occupational therapist. How I enjoyed that; I could not wait until the next morning to go again because the weaving was growing, even if I was pulling the edges in. I started to weave a floor rug and I told The Dragon that I wanted to be a weaver. 'Nonsense,' she said, 'no-one could make a living at that.' 'I can,' I said, 'and Mother is going to help me.' She would not listen so I took myself up to the superintendent's office. He was an ex sea captain, now in a wheelchair himself, and he understood through my tears that I was beginning to feel a failure since I had been there some time, while others had been coming in and going out into the world. He asked me what I wanted to do. I said 'weaving'. 'Why not?' he replied.

A few days later, I remember being told that Dorset County Council had agreed that this is what I should do, and they would lend me the money to buy a loom. The following week, Mother came and spent it with us, learning how to make and thread the warp on the loom, a mammoth task that I could never do. I stayed there a little longer, while Mother returned home, bought an old hen house and converted it into a workshop. The loom and I arrived home. So began another era of my life, I was home again and in my own workshop, not yet 18.

Battles over transport

Weaving became a good business for me as I was able to sell my products at local fêtes and fairs. However, for independence I needed transport and I had outgrown the various tricycles that I had used and my hips were wearing out and walking becoming more difficult when I was in my twenties. We bought an electric carriage in 1951 at the cost of £320 (a lot of money then). It was an Argson, and had a hood with windshield, apron, lights, horn and mirror, every-thing you could think of. We bought the carriage really to prove that I could use it, for it was at the time when the government began to issue motor chairs and electric carriages to disabled people. Everyone else was getting them, why not me? These were issued by the then Ministry of Health. I like others applied for one, was assessed by a man who took one look at me and mentally said 'hopeless'. Since I had ridden six tricycles, which had got bigger as I got bigger, for over 20 years, I knew a little about road sense and was determined to have a go at this. A letter arrived the next day, refusing me any help from the ministry in providing me with anything. So we scraped together the money to buy one ourselves.

I spent the following ten weeks doing nothing but driving around in it, with poor Mother on her bicycle behind me. I never knew what she would have done to prevent me from going under a bus. (This was Father's reaction as soon as he saw me sat in it.) One day, thinking I was alone and sailing along quite happily, I looked in the mirror to turn right across a busy street and there was Mum just behind me. I think this was the last time she followed me. After that I put in for the driving test that I would now have to take. It was ten years to the day after buying 'Monty', as it had been christened. I had my test with a nice young man and I did all he asked me to do correctly and I went home with my certificate to get a driving licence. He could not understand why I had been refused a ministry carriage and told me to apply again.

This I did. Then the fun or fight began. The same man who had refused me came and was very surprised to learn that I had a driving licence and he said, 'In that case we will have to grant you one.' But I already had a new carriage. No! They would not buy it from me to become their property, to maintain and supply new batteries when needed. So in due course, a reconditioned one arrived, the same, but for me it was different because the controls were positioned differently. This caused me problems having just got used to the other one. The man laughed about this, and said, 'I told you so', and pointed out that often he had to drive different cars. This annoyed me. (He wasn't disabled, was he?) Three times I went out in it, and three times had to be rescued by Mum and my brother Derek who had to chase off on the motorbike to get me home. Then someone referred the story of my two chairs to an MP who took this piece of bureaucracy gone mad to the then Prime Minister, Winston Churchill. After a while, I won, and it was settled by a £100 cheque and the carriage was maintained for the next 20-odd years. I went miles and miles, quite safely and happily, in my 'Monty' in those 20 years.

It wasn't until Mother had learned to drive and we were now living alone that laws were passed giving a private car allowance for disabled people as an alternative to the provision of invalid carriages. This was before the mobility allowance. We could not claim both the allowance and have an invalid carriage. So dear old Monty was taken away to be broken up and destroyed. I was told then that many other spastic people were given these electric carriages and even motor chairs after my fight.

Conclusion

This chapter has given a brief account of my early life. I have also written a longer account of my life that I hope to have published one day. My mother died in 1998 when she was 91. I wrote the following poem about her and our relationship that was both loving and stormy as we resisted together and apart.

My mum has been with me right through life
Has cared for me through trouble and strife
She has always been there, struggles to share
No matter what happens she shows that she cares

Now that she is old and needs help herself
She will not give in or let me down
It is me she thinks about before herself
Whatever the trouble she is always around

For sixty-seven years that has come and gone
It is Mum that has been around
To help me, to encourage me to overcome
So many struggles through life we have won

Walking and talking was the first
As my disability showed that was to get worse
A cabbage they said, your daughter would be
But Mum knew best and stood by me

She gave all she had, in money and kind
Anything to show that it wasn't my mind
That was damaged that day at the moment of birth
Nothing was good enough for me on this earth

My hand control, speech problems or walking
She soon was to get me talking
Without help or advice, there was no-one out there
She battled away with her love and her care

To help me to fight with all of her might, to show them all
That we could win through whatever befalls
Mum would work with those hands that was all that she had
Now she is alone and lonely, which is very sad

From the day I was born she has never been free
As Mum has given her life for me
Work, work, and work she would never shirk
A few more pence would buy something to stop my jerks

To prove to one and all how I have grown
To live independently on my own
How things have changed in such a way
That I am living alone today

No matter what happens, happy or sad
Some days are good – some days are bad
Like everyone else I take each day
To work itself out, come what may

Many years has gone by since I wrote this rhyme
More than ninety has gone by in time
For Mum who is still living alone
We still see each other or contact by phone

I have now been living in a purpose-built bungalow for wheelchair users in Milton Keynes for over 15 years with the minimum of daily help from carers and friends who only do what I am unable to do myself; I ask them to carry out my ideas with their steady hands for me which often only takes a few minutes. (In other words I make the bullets and they follow.) I am able to pay for having a good cooked dinner every day, no meals on wheels thank you, which I can pop in the microwave to warm up when I fancy it! I use a water heater over the sink to safely make my hot drinks any time of day or night.

At almost 76 my days are often not long enough. I spend many hours every day at my computers enjoying being able to write and explore the internet in every way possible. Writing has always been my biggest and I like to think my only handicap today. I not only write, but also attend college on one day each week, where I receive a lot of help and encouragement in taking computer courses one after another and gaining certificates. I have been privileged to be invited to give Power Point illustrated talks to college staff and at conferences about various disabilities at the Open University.

5

Two Pioneers of Self-advocacy

Ray Loomis and Tom Houlihan

Paul Williams

Paul Williams tells the story of two Americans, Ray Loomis and Tom Houlihan. Both Ray and Tom were leading members of the early self-advocacy movement in America. Their stories are important because they show that it was people with learning difficulties themselves who began the self-advocacy movement. Ray and Tom were very important leaders and this chapter helps us to remember their work.

In the late 1960s in the city of Omaha in the American state of Nebraska, a group of parents and professionals founded a pioneer service. It aimed to bring back to Omaha all the people with learning difficulties living in the state institution – Beatrice State Home near Lincoln, almost 100 miles away from Omaha. The new service was based on extensive use of ordinary housing to accommodate people in small groups. It was known as ENCOR, the Eastern Nebraska Community Office of Retardation. The service became a model for similar developments elsewhere in North America and in other parts of the world, including Britain. An influential account of the service was published in Britain in the 1970s by the Campaign for the Mentally Handicapped, now known as Values into Action (Thomas, Firth and Kendall 1978).

In 1975 a self-advocacy group was started in Omaha, many of the members of which were recipients of the ENCOR service. The group saw itself as akin to the original pioneer ENCOR enterprise, and so it called itself 'Project Two', ENCOR being considered to be 'Project One'. This chapter recounts the stories of two of the founders of Project Two, Ray Loomis and Tom Houlihan.

The origins of self-advocacy groups of people with learning difficulties can be traced back to Scandinavia in the 1960s and Britain and America in the early 1970s (Williams and Shoultz 1982). In 1974 a conference of people with learning difficulties was held in the state of Oregon in the USA to stimulate the development of self-advocacy. One of the delegates said: 'We are tired of being seen first as handicapped or retarded or disabled. We want to be seen as people first.' A motion was passed to establish a statewide organization to promote self-advocacy, with the name 'People First'. The idea behind this name spread to other parts of the USA and eventually to Britain and other countries, so that many self-advocacy groups are now called 'People First'. In Omaha, Ray Loomis devised a saying that he would often quote to encourage people to express their views and to join Project Two: 'If you think you are handicapped, you may as well stay indoors. If you think you are a person first, come out and tell the world!' (Williams and Shoultz 1982, p.17).

Ray had been admitted to Beatrice State Institution in 1953 when he was in his late teens, after failing to perform well at his special school and getting into trouble with some other local youths. In the institution he was seen as a trouble-maker and he made several attempts to escape. He was often placed in seclusion as punishment. When he was finally released in 1968, after 15 years there, one of the doctors predicted that he would be back within three days. Although contact between the sexes was strictly limited and controlled, Ray had got to know a woman resident, Nancy, and they became fond of each other. Nancy remembers: 'Of course they wouldn't let you hold hands or anything, unless you could hide from them' (Williams and Shoultz 1982, p.49).

Ray lived in Lincoln when he got out. Nancy was released in 1969 and went to live in Omaha. Ray discovered this and decided to move to Omaha, where he and Nancy became partners. They married in 1974. Nancy worked as a maid in a hospital and Ray as a dishwasher in a restaurant. In 1977 they had a son, Billy. Ray got to know most of the people with learning difficulties who had come to Omaha from the state institution. He had the idea, which he called his 'brainstorm', to form a group that would meet to support each other. In 1975, with the help of some non-disabled friends, he held a meeting to start the group. Only three people turned up. But Ray persevered and held more meetings, and by the end of 1975 about 40 people had signed up. The group decided on the name 'Project Two', and later founded a statewide organization to support local groups, which they called 'People First Nebraska'.

Ray led Project Two, as its president, until he developed heart trouble in 1979. He underwent heart surgery, but tragically died from complications after the operation. At his funeral, which was packed with people from all over Nebraska, this eulogy was given by Ed Skarnulis, president of the local parents group, the Greater Omaha Association for Retarded Citizens:

> Knowing Ray Loomis was like being sure the sun would come up each morning. You could trust Ray when he said he'd do something. He loved to kid around and joke with people, and was a master at gently putting others in their proper place when they got a little too proud or a little too talkative. But behind the warmth of his laugh and the sparkle in his eye was a serious man who felt a sense of urgency. He knew that someone is sitting on a crowded institution ward somewhere waiting to come home. He knew that someone is staring at a TV set in an apartment, feeling lonely and desperately needing a friend to be with and to talk to.
>
> Ray was a dreamer, but he didn't just hope for dreams to come true. Ray said that when he started Project Two he was scared, but that didn't make him back away. He used to say that he was a person just like anybody else, but that we all have to stand up for ourselves. Standing up for ourselves is going to be hard without Ray Loomis to lean on. Nancy and Billy will need all the courage they have, and all the encouragement we can give. All of the members of Project Two and all of us who worked with Ray are going to be missing an important part of our lives without him. But we owe to Ray our best effort at standing up for others and ourselves and looking ahead to the future. We need to follow his footsteps, as people helping people. (Williams and Shoultz 1982, p.32–3)

One of the three people who attended the first meeting that Ray called to start Project Two was Tom Houlihan, a man with Down's Syndrome who had always lived in Omaha. He visited Britain in 1980 and travelled all over the country, sometimes unaccompanied, to talk to people about self-advocacy. He enjoyed his trip greatly, and always used to say, 'I left my heart in England.' During the early years of Project Two, Tom was vice-president, providing valuable support to Ray Loomis in getting the group established. Sadly, he too has since died, and here is the eulogy given at a memorial service for him by Shirley Dean, one of the advisers to Project Two:

Thomas J. Houlihan was born on the 12 January 1943 and died on the 27 October 1999 after a six-month illness. Tom will long be remembered as a spokesperson in the field of developmental disabilities, an advocate, a friend and a family member. He lived life to the fullest and made an impact on the hearts of many of us. Described by his friends as fun, outgoing, exuberant, thoughtful and big-hearted, Tom had a twinkle in his eyes, a smile on his face, and lots of ideas. Tom was a founder member of Project Two, the first self-advocacy group of people with developmental disabilities in Nebraska. Project Two held the first statewide convention in 1978, at which Tom was a speaker and leader. This was the exciting beginning of People First of Nebraska. Since then, self-advocacy groups have started across the state and conventions have become an annual event, loved by all who attend.

Tom was an advocate: he spoke up for himself, his peers and his friends. He testified before county commissioners and legislators. He helped educate people about issues that are important to people with developmental disabilities and about the abilities people have. He set an example of what a person with developmental disabilities could accomplish which was an inspiration to others. He also had a gift for making people feel comfortable. At a speaking engagement in South Dakota, Tom asked to be the first speaker. He interacted with the audience of 600 people and set the crowd at ease, as well as other speakers. On another occasion, Tom stood up in front of about 200 people and spoke to the board of directors about a decision he disagreed with. He had planned his strategy himself and did not share it with anyone ahead of time. He had his cousin come to stand up with him at the meeting where he said he was going to resign as a client if the decision was not reversed.

Tom was a truly important member of his community. He was known throughout the community and his life touched the lives of many people from all walks of life. He was a devoted member of St Cecilia's Cathedral Church, and later St Pius Xth Church. He was a proud member of the Knights of Columbus for many years. Tom had a job working at the St Vincent de Paul Society for 31 years. He was a leader in Project Two and a friend to many people. Tom's family was very important to him. He lived with his mother and took care of her when her health began to fail. Later, he lived in an apartment by himself or with a roommate. Tom often spoke of his brother Denny, who provided help and support to Tom throughout the years. Tom spoke with pride when he talked about his brother and his brother's children. Denny has also expressed the joy of living with Tom. He described him as an upbeat person who had a wonderful life.

When people came to Nebraska from other countries to see the community-based services for people with developmental disabilities, they met Tom and visited his apartment. When Bonnie Shoultz and I began planning a trip to England, people asked there if Tom could come with us. Tom was asked to come to England because of his accomplishments, his speaking abilities and the way he lived his life. Tom raised many issues there. He also fell in love with England. We all had a wonderful trip. Bonnie remembers the first time she met Tom. She had just started working at ENCOR. She went to two Christmas parties on the same day. The first was a formal affair where she felt very uncomfortable. From there she went to the second party at a friend's house, where she had a great time dancing with this exuberant guy Tom Houlihan. She felt she was where she belonged, and she and Tom became great friends. Years later, Tom was talking with a state senator and he asked if a law could be passed to enable people to adopt brothers and sisters. Tom wanted to adopt Bonnie as his sister. Tom always came up with ideas.

It is important in charting and recording the history of the self-advocacy movement that we do not give all the credit to the non-disabled helpers, supporters and advisers, or merely acknowledge the researchers and academics who have written about it. Those who initiated the movement and gave it the strength and worldwide coverage that it has today were people with learning difficulties themselves, many of whom had had traumatic experiences of oppression and rejection. Ray Loomis and Tom Houlihan are two examples of these pioneers of the exciting and powerful development of self-advocacy.

References

Thomas, D., Firth, H. and Kendall, A. (1978) *ENCOR: A Way Ahead.* London: Campaign for the Mentally Handicapped (now Values into Action).

Williams, P. and Shoultz, B. (1982) *We Can Speak for Ourselves: Self-advocacy by Mentally Handicapped People.* London: Souvenir Press.

6

'I've Had Enough of the Everyday Thing'
Karen Spencer's Life Story

Karen Spencer with Jan Walmsley

Karen Spencer talks about her childhood and her difficult relationship with her family. Karen left home when she was 16 and had a troubled early adult life that included sleeping rough and living in a detention centre for a while. Karen moved to Northampton and became involved in People First. She became Chair of Central England People First. She talks about the difficulties of Chairing People First and explains how the organization is developing. Karen tells us how she has had to become involved in complaints as well as disputes with other organizations. Karen looks to the future and wants to do more work with computers, training and research.

Introduction

Karen Spencer has been a leading figure in English self-advocacy since the early 1990s. This is an account of her life and the work she has done in the

self-advocacy movement. The material from this chapter is based on two interviews conducted by Jan Walmsley with Karen Spencer. What follows are Karen's
words interspersed with some of Jan's own comments that are designed to
provide background and to help explain the story. In order to make quite clear
whose words are whose we will start each section with initials (JW or KS). This
technique helps ensure that when we use dialogue directly from the interviews we
do not have to break up the sections with explanatory notes. The chapter is partly
a life story, and in this it represents a personal story of resistance against stereo-
typing and control. However, it is also more than a life story in that it provides an
insight into the growth of collective resistance in the form of the organization
called 'People First' which brings together people with learning difficulties to
campaign for their own services and for the control of their own lives. Karen has
been involved with People First as it has grown and begun to grapple with many
of the tensions inherent in organizations when they have to deal with the management of staff, budgets and interpersonal differences.

Childhood and family

JW   Karen's learning difficulties are not specific. This has created some
      difficulties for her. Here she describes how she discovered she had
      learning difficulties and the response of her family, particularly her
      mother.

KS   I was born in Manchester in 1963. I had a mum and a dad, a brother
      and a sister. I was the middle one of three. My sister was the oldest, my
      brother was the youngest. I started out at a normal school, St
      Augustine's, then I was at White Moss till I was seven, then I was
      moved to Ten Acres, another special school, that's from 7 till 16.
            My mum says I failed a test or something, that's why I was moved,
      and St Augustine's wouldn't have me back because I'd spent a year at
      special school. White Moss was good. Ten Acres was just a special
      school so what you did in one class you did in the others. They tried. I
      learnt to read and write, yeah, but we were all at different levels. I think
      I was classed as mentally subnormal. Me mum told me I think. No, I
      wasn't told, I read it in my file. But the trouble was I was born
      prematurely so I hadn't developed as a normal child anyway. I also got
      whooping cough when I was 18 months. That set me back a bit, my
      immune system. I had whooping cough worse than my brother and my
      sister, and I wasn't discharged from hospital when they were. It was

never actually proved that that was the reason [for not developing as a 'normal' child].

The problem was I had an able sister. My sister was 'normal' as the saying is. The problem was because my disability wasn't noticeable it was proven that I was messing around and that I was just lazy. That was my mum's view anyway.

JW Karen's memories of her relationships with her family have a continuing theme of injustice, unfairness, something which seems to motivate her even today.

KS I can't remember what it was like when I was living at home, not as a child, no. I can't remember what it was like younger than seven.

My mum didn't get on with me. She hit me a few times. The way she treated me but she didn't treat the others. My mum didn't have any right to think I was different, well not half the time, maybe a third of the time. Like if I got a good school report I had to prove that the teachers were lying. Once I got a school report saying I was good at maths so she had to prove that was a lie. By setting me a maths problem. She didn't tell me how to do it. It's her generation isn't it? My mum's older than you.

Can't remember Dad. I think he came about twice to see me when I was at home. He didn't see any of us. He didn't want to know, right, he didn't want to know us, he had our stepmother so.

I didn't get on with my brother and sister, they didn't get on with me and I didn't get on with them. My mum made me feel unsafe because she found ways to upset me. For 20 years I was blamed for my brother's ear. When my dad was living at home I tripped my brother up and instead of hitting me he hit my brother and perforated his eardrum. For 20 years I was blamed for that by her. So it was living with the guilt when you are getting blamed for that on a regular basis. That was about the last time I lived at home.

I didn't have friends just because of my mum. I wasn't allowed to go out. Sister went out when she was older. I didn't challenge Mum with it, didn't even ask her. There's no point arguing, not even asking. I don't know why, it's just the way she was. It wasn't the discipline though, my sister tried to get the blame on me for smashing the window. My sister thought I was stupid and was going to take the blame for it. I started to pay for the window, which was a bit annoying. Why should I pay for the window if I didn't break it? Probably to teach me a lesson but it's not a nice lesson is it? I save my money up, then I have to pay for it. I wasn't even around when it got smashed. I was on the toilet. I wasn't allowed to watch cartoons because she said I was too old to watch them, but what gets me is my sister was allowed to watch them. Last time I saw her was when I was 17 or 18. Haven't seen my brother since I was 21, no 20.

Leaving home

JW The differences within the family led to conflict, and to Karen leaving home aged 16.

KS When I was 16 I was put in a remand home. I was refusing to go home, sleeping rough. I just walked out. There was a reason that I couldn't cope any more with the way she was treating me and never allowed to go out. It was like when I left school I had to get a job or she was shipping me off to me dad. They'd been separated since I was two on and off and then when I was 12 they got divorced, but she said right if I got a job I could stay at home, so I took the first job, trainee handbag-maker, peanuts, wouldn't get you anything these days. I got sacked. I wouldn't go in one day so they sacked me. I refused to go into work because they decided to lock me up in the lift. It was the sort of stunts they were doing which I didn't agree with. They had this thing that I had to sweep up because I was the new one. And I said no, and then they locked me in the lift, which I didn't think was very funny. I think I got arrested because it was the only way not to be allowed to go back home.

While I was living at home I had no money to spend, my benefits from the DHSS [Department of Health and Social Security] went straight to her. As soon as she got my wage packet I was having to pay £15 rent, £5 bus fare, that only left me with one pound odd. Now when my sister got a job she was given two weeks to find a job and then she had a week before she had to pay. She had a lot more money than me. I was only earning £21 a week. If I didn't clock in early I'd have only got £19.

They cautioned me. Vandalizing a wall that was coming down anyway. So really I was just helping it along. I went back home for two weeks, but it got so bad me mum had me seeing a psychologist. She said I had a behaviour problem because she didn't understand why I didn't want that particular job. Why didn't she work there then? So before I seen the psychologist I was on my way, I was out two days, long enough. And I told the police I wasn't going back home and if they took me back I'd run. I went to a children's home for a day, then they put me in a detention centre, because you're 16, no-one's going to take you because you are not old enough to have a flat.

No it weren't fun but it were safe.

JW   Leaving home and falling out with her family led to a very unstable period, with experience of a whole variety of placements, none of which was entirely satisfactory. Unfairness and injustice continue to be themes of Karen's story.

KS   First time I was there at the detention centre for about a month, from there I moved into a foster home. I lasted one day, I was 16, her daughter was telling her to f– off, she was 14 coming in all hours, I was 16 I had to be in by nine o'clock. But her daughter was f–ing and blinding at 11 at night, and the house was full of kids screaming all night, so then I went off to a children's home. I went back to Burford [detention centre] three times. They made decisions, they didn't ask me what the problem was, they didn't get down to the problem. Then they stopped me going home like, 'cos my mum asked me to go home for the day, and they wouldn't let me; they got me really annoyed because they said I couldn't go home, then they said they wouldn't let me go, then they apologized when I challenged them.

When I was 16 I went to Pengwern Hall, it wasn't a nice place because the staff were allowed to hit you which they shouldn't have been I know now. I didn't know that then. You got members of staff watching TV, they weren't allowed to watch TV but when I asked them nicely if they could move so I could watch TV they got really nasty and gave me a hiding.

If you were a girl you got to do the housework. Boys did the outside work. 'Cos I liked doing the outside work they let me work outside in the afternoon.

My mum didn't care less where I was living. If she did she wouldn't have let me live there because it's not the sort of place any kid should go to. Now it's for students of a certain age but it wasn't then.

I actually moved out after nine months to a social services house for physically unable, but that's not the place I wanted to go, I wanted to go to Chester 'cos that was where my friends were, but because of money and because I had family in Manchester I wasn't allowed. There were about 30 people living there, it wasn't the place I wanted to be. You had to lock your door because people would wander in and take your things. I came into my room one day and all my pictures of Police had been taken off the wall. Then I went to Nacro hostel, have you heard of it? [Nacro is a crime reduction charity.] That was worse. There were all sorts there, drug addicts, and I went out for a walk with one of them and he tried to get me joyriding with him.

While I was living at the Nacro hostel I got assessed to move into a Jewish home, a Jewish organization, not Jewish staff. I had friends there and I knew the people I'd be living with. She [Mum] didn't like Jewish people I don't think. I mean it's not like I made the decision, the decisions were made. I had my assessments, I was interviewed, my mum was even involved in the interviews, it's not like she wasn't involved. But she said the decision was mine, it wasn't the decision she wanted.

JW   Karen's relationship with her mother continued to be difficult, made more complicated by her mother developing a relationship with another man. From Karen's point of view, her mother was not behaving as mothers should.

KS   When I moved to that Nacro hostel my mum had decided to see me. She had no job, that was the only reason, and to screw up my life by saying she was sorry and all that, then when it suited her to get a job then suddenly just dump me. 'Cos it wasn't the problem she had the job; the problem was she was only seeing me for less than an hour. It's like suddenly she got that job and the contact I had with her was non-existent. I rang her up, she wasn't at home. I rang another day, she wasn't at home. You know, so it was the stage she had me in her life till it suited her if you know what I mean. She works at the hospital, as a cleaner, or I don't know.

We had this falling out in 1987. I decided to write a letter that she thought more of the job than she did of me, and it just went from there. What she did was, when I moved from the Nacro hostel to Harper Way I wasn't far away. And she chose when to see me. It was always on her terms. And when I would go home to see her, she decided. If you're going to make amends then she needs to treat you with a bit more respect. I was only allowed to go home when she said. It's not just going home, it's having a time to get there and leave by.

I was 21 when I fought her.

As soon as she got the letter she wrote one back, mine was tame to what she wrote. I just wrote that she thought more of the job than she did of me because there wasn't any compromise. If she'd said as she got the job she wouldn't be seeing me, that would have been fair enough.

But she never said, right, she wasn't going to see me again. It was like the job came first and that was it. But when I was going home, like if she had a guest, it was like I had to go. I mean parents shouldn't do that. They either take you as you are or not at all. I mean I did see her on the bus when I was babysitting and when I went out on Boxing Day, I did see her on the bus. She was with this guy; she might have married him by now. She used to go out with another man then she said they were getting married and I said 'Where do I stand on this?' I mean she said like if she actually married him it would be up to him when I saw her. Now he's not my dad so I don't understand why he'd have a say when I saw my mum.

I wrote one letter, she wrote one back. That was it.

I did try to ring a few times, but it came to nothing, it wasn't worth the grief. Then they knocked the house down so I don't know where she is living. I think she's still alive. Before I moved here she was.

I haven't got any pictures of my mum. Me mum ripped them up. Last thing I know my brother was still living at home, and my sister sees her, it's only me that's not allowed to.

Involvement in People First

JW   After this major falling out with her mum, Karen moved to Northampton with a friend, Daniel. She rapidly gained prominence in what was then Northampton People First. She is currently Chair of the enlarged Central England People First [CEPF] that embraces five self-advocacy organizations in central England and one in Devon. As Chair of this complex federated organization, Karen carries considerable responsibilities, unpaid.

KS   The organization's growing, growing to a stage when it's too big. There's only been 18 months of the nine years I been here that I haven't been an officer. Me, Ian and Nigel are feeling we are getting bogged down. But if we make changes, Ian and Nigel could be out of a job. We want to concentrate on particular things, like training, consultancy, and I want to concentrate on the internet, training and research. For me Ian and Nigel, it's been the same people and I've had enough of the everyday thing. I cannot do the internet work because there is always something else. And I don't think it's fair, I'm getting bogged down, cranky you know.

It's like when you go home you are still thinking about the day. Like specially with the funding. N [one of CEPF's supporters] kept pressuring me to make the decision about who was going to be made redundant. Now that's difficult 'cos it would be J or R, right. I mean J's OK, A's OK, I get on pretty well with R. It would have had to be last one in you see. I think that's what most employers do, don't they? In the end we decided it was too difficult to choose so we decided to make everyone redundant. Luckily funding came in and we didn't have to do it.

It would be really hard to make people redundant. Like N has been a good friend to people in People First for ten years. I know I can ring him if I have a problem with my computer...and when are we going to the pictures. He spent hours sorting my new mail system out last night.

I think with me, I've had enough of it. Janet was Chair for a year and I was elected Vice-Chair, but when we were having the financial problems, you know, she disappeared, so I was dumped with that, and then I got re-elected as Chair at the AGM. I sign the cheques. I decide who gets sacked and who gets employed. It stinks when you have to do that. And disciplining. Last time I had to suspend Linda. That was not nice, considering I'd had no training.

There isn't any rewards is there? I just get a lot of grief. Even if I wasn't Chair I'd get the trips abroad.

The supporter can't do it, because it's an organization controlled and run by people with learning difficulties, so if we got a support person to do it, that would be wrong. The supporters do what we ask them to do.

JW   But could you not ask him to do it? You are the boss.

KS   They wouldn't do it, because it's not that simple.

JW   Within People First issues around who does the support for particular people in particular activities can be especially tricky. One incident recounted by Karen illustrates this. Names have been anonymized.

KS   Because he had been ill Roger needed someone to actually support him, to take him to hospital, then to drive him to a very important meeting in London, because he was still under the hospital then. And the thing is he chose someone, Jill, and she agreed, and he was happy because he wanted someone he knew. She supports him in that but then he decides he wants her on a regular basis, so last week he asked me to send an email saying he didn't want her to support him on the

Monday. Well we sent an email on the Sunday. The thing is, he should have done it himself, but he didn't want to offend her. We know she got the email because we received the confirmed thing, but she turned up on the Monday so he went along with it, and didn't tell her he had N lined up. So when N arrived Roger just told him he didn't want him. Well you can imagine N's feelings, if you travel all the way to London on the train just to be told you're not wanted. Now N wants to express his feelings to Roger, and you know who's going to be piggy in the middle. Because I am N's line manager. It's not what I want but Roger's requested the meeting between me, him and N. Roger's told this other person he's got this predicament, and he wants me to take him out of it but it's not my mess really.

When I first did the Chair it was just Northampton, and that was OK. But now…

JW   Central England People First is a federated organization. Northampton was the original People First, but it has overseen the development of other groups in the South, West and East Midlands. The relationship between these groups is not always straightforward, and as Chair Karen has to deal with some of the conflicts.

KS   I've had enough of management. Been there, got the T-shirt. I think it's the grief you get from the other organizations. Maybe they don't like that we are getting on better than they are.

I don't think it's that the two organizations can't get on, it's the people. I think the supporter pushes too far, pushing people to do things. It's like there was some money on offer from the council to benefit people with learning difficulties in Blanktown so we came up with this brilliant idea to do information. And they [the other group] said no, all we want is a company car. They are saying they don't want to do it. So if they don't want to do it, we'll do it.

JW   But it is Blanktown's money?

KS   No, our money, because they did not get the money. They turned it down because they want a company car. How's that going to benefit people with learning difficulties in Blanktown, unless they belong to People First? They didn't like the idea, so we are going to take it on and fund it ourselves.

It was fair, we were thinking about the people in Blanktown, not just People First. That's what the council were giving the money for.

JW   But I remember being there when you came up with the idea about how to spend the money. No-one from Blanktown PF was there.

KS   But we sent them straight an email, and they were on the phone. But whatever we did they wanted a company car.

We've got three company cars. But we do more travel than them. They think just getting it is it. It needs petrol, tax, maintenance. We won't maintain it. Once their funding's gone they need to get more funding. They can't keep using Northampton's funding, but that's what's happened. We've been getting money out of reserves, and I'm thinking we are not doing all this work just to support Blanktown, just because we helped start them up.

JW   As Chair of the federated organizations that comprise Central England People First, Karen has to deal with complaints. Here she describes one recent incident.

KS   People won't work with Hughtown because of the abuse they get, no-one wants to do anything for them. I've seen the Chair get really out of hand, making another committee member cry, and he's a grown man. He sees his sister sometimes, not frequent, so she wanted to go out with him for the day, and he said he was going to miss the meeting, which is fair enough, and she [the Hughtown Chair] goes 'You f–ing can't' as if he had no rights to actually do that. And he's a full-sized guy. If she can do that to him...

As Chair, I have to deal with complaints which is not such a good idea. We just sit here and make a judgement. I went down there and got the information, but that's as far as it went. No follow-up. There's nothing we can do. No-one is willing to actually say what happened, there's no evidence. I'd have suspended her for a couple of weeks. They are quick enough to do that to other people. And I'm thinking why aren't they doing that with her, just because she's Chair.

JW   People with learning difficulties are not always considerate of other minority groups. Karen states her position on this.

KS   I said I'd never forgive Lianna [Chair of Kirktown PF] for her comments about gay people. When we did the White Paper Conference she was being rude about black people which then sparked off Patrick which then sparked off Katriona because they are black people. It's all to do with generations again isn't it? To actually not be racist if your parents are racist. My uncle was racist against black people, didn't mean

I was going to be. My mum was racist against Jewish people, didn't mean I was going to be. When you know what your parents are saying is wrong, that's your choice.

I don't think Lianna was referring to me when she was rude about gay people. But it was the fact she said it in front of Jack (who is gay) that really sparked me off. I could have said 'You are being fat and ugly'. It's not that she is ugly, but she is fat, you know what I mean, don't you? She'd be really offended if anyone said that to her.

Education and future

JW Karen has always struggled with finding the right place for herself in the education system. Here she explains how she wants to develop her internet skills, and reflects on the need for support and some of the frustrations of being placed in special needs provision.

KS Even now I don't think I'm making progress. Everyone says I am. I'm not sure what my difficulties are. Concentration. I do have problems with reading and writing but not much. I can type with two fingers. If I had voice-activated software it might be easier.

Reason I want to look for an internet course I want to benefit and gain my experience also. I did do a computer course with an ET [Employment Training] scheme – you know what those are? Well they said we had to sit a maths test, me and Daniel before, just because we had learning difficulties. The other ones didn't have to do it. Really annoying. They were using a program called Wordstar, a word-processing thing. It was typing. It was not what I wanted to do, secretary work, and just because I wasn't as quick as the others they put me in the dunce's class. I'm not stupid. I know what the dunce's class is. I know who was in that class, people who couldn't be bothered. So they had me doing things like making a cup of tea. Making cups of tea, what's that got to do with computers? I had to write an essay like you had to put it in stages like putting a teabag in a cup, putting the milk in... Then they had me imagine I was building a shelf. Then I thought since I was imagining, maybe I'd put in a blank sheet of paper if I'm imagining it. Well then they had me doing an essay about how to light a lamp.

It's always put me off doing a course. It's not like I can't do the work on the computer, it's if there is written work I need help. If I've got to take notes and things like that. If I can do it all on the computer, but I'll still need help with the questions.

I don't like going into a class with people with learning difficulties because I know what my limits are but when I'm in a class with people who are slower than me, then I'm not going to get anything out of it. When they put me in a foundation course at college they put me in Module 2 doing the basic stuff, which I could already do, and for 40 minutes I'm still sitting there bored out of my brain. And she goes 'Read a book' and I says 'They're baby books'.

I like being in mixed groups where there's different people doing different things. Like with Chris, he can't read very well, but he's good at other things. When we were doing the video course Rachel was supporting us but she had to disappear on the last day when there was written work. And if I wasn't Chris's friend I'd have left him to struggle, so what I did, I was trying to do mine and his at the same time, but it became a problem, I can't do mine and his. So I did his, and took it home and put it in my folder.

I might try college but it's a question of transport. It's a problem where colleges are. I can only get to Wellingborough, living in Wellingborough and having it publicized I have learning difficulties might not be such a good idea.

Well I'm in my own house now, aren't I. I've got two cats. They have been out since your dog's been here. But maybe I've had enough of doing the everyday thing. It's not like I haven't done it. I want to concentrate on the computer work training and research.

7

Resilience and Resistance in the Life Histories of Three Women with Learning Difficulties in Iceland

Gudrún Stefánsdóttir and Rannveig Traustadóttir

This is the story of three women who lived in an institution in Iceland. All show examples of resistance and individual strength. The women refused to accept the labels that they had been given. They also kept their own memories from before they lived in an institution alive. Their families and friends were an important link to the past. The stories show that the women did not simply accept what was done to them but fought to maintain their own individuality.

Introduction

In Iceland, as in other countries, many people with learning difficulties born during the first half of the twentieth century were removed from their families and sent to long-stay institutions. Some were taken from their families as children and grew up in institutional settings confined to the powerful regime of the institution where others controlled their lives, set the rules and made the decisions. How did people cope with such experiences? What day-to-day strategies did they employ to survive? Did they resist their circumstances or surrender to the power of the institution? This chapter addresses these questions through examining the experiences of three women who spent parts of their lives in institutions. They are members of a women's history group established as a collaborative forum for women with learning difficulties to come together to share their life histories. The women's history group is a part of a larger life history project with people with learning difficulties. The study is Gudrún Stefánsdóttir's doctoral research carried out at the University of Iceland under the supervision of and in collaboration with Rannveig Traustadóttir. In this chapter we tell the stories of three of the women in the history group and examine signs of resilience and resistance in their lives. First, however, we describe the women's history group.

The women's history group

In recent years scholars in the field of learning disability have developed inclusive life history methods based on cooperation and a close relationship between the researcher and the participants (Atkinson 1997, 2004; Booth and Booth 1996; Stalker 1998; Traustadóttir and Johnson 2000; Walmsley and Johnson 2003; Ward 1998). One example of this work has involved establishing groups where researchers and people with learning difficulties collaborate. These groups provide a forum for people with learning difficulties to talk about their lives, recall memories, discuss the research process, give advice about the study and participate in the collection and analysis of the data (Atkinson 1997; Atkinson, Jackson and Walmsley 1997; Rolph 2002; Walmsley and Johnson 2003).

As a part of Gudrún's doctoral work she established a research group with four of the women who took part in the larger study. The group was called 'The women's history group' and met once a week from September 2003 to May 2004. The group has met once a month since the autumn of 2004 and will continue working together after the dissertation research is over. The group wants to teach others about collaborative life history work and keep working on these kinds of projects in the future. Three of the women in the group lived in institutions for people with learning difficulties and it is their experiences that provides the basis for this chapter.

The aim of the women's history group was to gain a deeper understanding of the women's stories and give them the opportunity to discuss their feelings and experiences with other women who had backgrounds similar to their own. The group recognized the importance of letting the voices of people with learning difficulties be heard in research and writing. We were aware of the fact that these voices have hardly been heard, neither historically nor in the present (Atkinson and Walmsley 1999). Many scholars have found that participation in life history work can have a strong emancipating effect on people with learning difficulties and for many it has proven to be a fruitful way to cope with difficult life experiences, for example life in an institution (Atkinson 2004; Goodley 2000; Rolph 2002; Stefánsdóttir 2004; Walmsley and Johnson 2003). One of the topics discussed in the group is the women's experiences of their participation in the research and what effect it has had on them.

Every fourth meeting the group has invited guests who in some way were connected to the women's lives. The objective was to give the women opportunities to discuss particular memories and to deepen the exploration of events in their past. The women also felt it was important to hear the opinions of others and, at the same time, they had lots of questions they wanted answered. They took turns in deciding whom to invite but in most cases these were people everyone in the group knew and who had touched their lives at some point in time. For example, the woman who was director of the institution where two of the women had lived was invited to come and participate in the group's discussion about life in the institution and to answer their questions.

The group has on a few occasions been asked to give talks about the work in the group. Each of these times two women, a researcher and a woman with learning difficulties, give presentations and the women with learning difficulties have taken turns participating in this. Mostly these talks have been in university courses that train students to work with disabled people. One of the women has also taken part in an international collaboration in which scholars and people with learning difficulties work together in research.

The three women

Below are brief versions of the life histories of the three women. After their stories we will discuss signs of resilience and the strategies the women used to survive the institution and other difficult experiences. We also examine if and how the women resisted or protested the situation they found themselves in. In accordance to the women's wishes their real names are used in the chapter.

Erla: Mediator and advocate

Erla Magnúsdóttir was born in 1935 in Reykjavík. Her family was poor and when she was nine months old she was sent to the paediatric ward at the University Hospital in Reykjavík to have an operation. She was born with physical and visual impairments, and the doctors said she needed surgery. The operation was never performed. Erla, however, lived in the paediatric ward until she was nine years old. The poverty of her family and the dominant attitudes of the time, which included regarding disabled people as patients, were probably the reasons for her staying in hospital for such a long time. Erla returned home to her family in 1945 and lived there for two years. When she was 11 she was sent to an institution for people with learning difficulties out in the country. Erla was not given a wheel-chair till she had been in the institution for a few years and, although she had a visual impairment, she did not obtain a pair of glasses until she was 35 years old. Erla says that when she was a child she had no idea she was labelled as 'mentally retarded' (as it was called at the time). She first found out about that label after she was put in the institution.

Erla lived in institutions for 38 years and, as she says herself, never liked it and never felt good being there. Erla moved into a group home in 1993. Now she lives in a small group home for senior citizens with learning difficulties and works at a rehabilitation centre. She is happy with her life today and says with pleasure that for the first time she has her own home. Although Erla has spent most of her life in institutions she is a fighter and has always maintained her dignity and self-respect. Her story reflects the fact that she cares deeply about those who are less able and has a history of speaking up on behalf of herself and others.

In the history group Erla plays the role of a mediator. When the women do not agree Erla steps in and mediates. She is close to 70 years old and is a gentle woman and at the same time is full of good will and interest in life. She is neither angry nor bitter, despite the difficult life she has had, and she enjoys life to the fullest. Erla is a great lover of music and art and sings in a choir. She often goes to the Kringlan and Kolaport shopping malls. In 1993 she became a founding member of Átak, the Icelandic self-advocacy group, and she continues to be an active member.

Ingiborg: Poet and nature lover

Ingiborg Eide Geirsdóttir was born in 1950 in a small fishing village. She grew up with her family until she was nine years old, when she was sent to an institution far from her village. She lived in the institution for 22 years. Ingiborg was born with twisted legs and, like Erla, she didn't know she had been labelled as 'mentally retarded' until she was sent to the institution. Ingiborg was sterilized in 1981. She was offered a place in one of the first group homes in Iceland but on the condition that she was sterilized before she left the institution.

Today Ingiborg lives in her own flat on the basement floor of the group home. She has worked in the same place since 1976 – a large hospital laundry – is exceedingly proud of her job and speaks of herself as a 'working woman'. Ingiborg writes poetry and has had a poem published in a large Icelandic newspaper. Being a nature lover, she enjoys being outside and travelling around Iceland. She thinks it is good to live alone but cultivates friendships by inviting her friends and family now and then for coffee and a cake.

Ingiborg is a creature of habit. Her life is orderly and she likes to keep to her routine and always do the same things at the same time. She did, however, alter her habits to meet with the study group despite the fact that normally she would have been doing something else at the time the group meets. This is a sign that she greatly values her participation in the group. One of her valuable contributions has been her unbelievably good memory of dates of events that have been discussed in the group.

Eygló Ebba: The pioneer

Eygló Ebba Hreinsdóttir was born in Reykjavík in 1950. She grew up with her parents, brothers and sisters and went to an ordinary school. She was born with a physical impairment but, as she says, was not labelled 'handicapped' until she was sent to an institution. Ebba was sterilized when she was 14 years old, the operation being performed under the pretext of removing her appendix. When Ebba was 18 her mother became ill and died. Following her mother's death Ebba was sent to an institution for people with learning difficulties and lived there for eight years. She moved out of the institution in 1976 to a group home, together with six other inmates from the institution. She worked in a sheltered workshop from 1975 to 1993, but has not worked outside the home since then. Ebba married in 1993 and lives with her husband in a rented flat that is part of a public housing scheme. They travel a great deal, both in Iceland and abroad, enjoy the theatre, go often to the Kringlan shopping mall, downtown, and 'do what people do', as Ebba phrases it. She is content with her life today and feels that a great deal has been achieved for people with learning difficulties. She looks at herself as a pioneer in the field of learning difficulties in Iceland, both because she was the first resident in the first group home in Reykjavík in 1976 and because of her participation in the study described in this chapter. She is an active member of an association fighting for the rights of disabled people.

Resistance and resilience in the women's stories

The women's stories all show examples of resistance and resilience but these are expressed in different ways. The women's stories were collected through individual interviews, group interviews and the collaborative work of the history group. A detailed analysis of all of this material and discussions with the women provided insights into the many and various ways the women had managed to survive the institutions and the different forms of resistance they used to protest the situation they found themselves in. Below we discuss the following: resistance to being labelled, the importance of memories, anger and sadness, friendships and relationships, and the importance to the women of telling their stories.

Resisting the label and the stigma

Research indicates that one reason for people's resistance and resilience is the importance of all humans to maintain their self-respect (Goodley 2000; King, Brown and Smith 2003). Most people who experience stigma, devaluation and humiliation feel the need to protest the situation they find themselves in. The three women have been labelled in various ways, being called 'mentally retarded', 'handicapped' or as having 'learning difficulties'. Such labels have often allowed society to ignore people's humanity and abilities. Influential theories about the effects of labelling and stigmatization were published as early as the 1960s (Becker 1963; Goffman 1961, 1963). These theories stated that the 'deviance' was socially created and that who is seen as 'different' is culturally determined. Inspired by these theories, scholars began to study their influence on the lives of people with learning difficulties (e.g. Edgerton 1967, Bogdan and Taylor 1982). US sociologist Erving Goffman (1963) published his famous study *Stigma* on how people coped with stigma in daily interactions with others. He concluded that those who were stigmatized often looked at themselves in the same negative light as others. Self-image and self-confidence suffered when people were not able to play the valued social roles usually awarded and recognized by the society in which they lived.

Stigmatization has had a decisive influence on the lives of the three women in this study. For example, they have all had to undergo sterilization, indicating that socially they have not been trusted to live a normal family life and have children. All three were institutionalized for extended periods of their lives. Ebba described how awful the years in the institution were. She was afraid, felt insecure and often landed in circumstances she could not control. Worst, however, was the experience of being labelled as 'mentally retarded'. Ebba often wished she was one of the young non-disabled women staff at the institution, many of whom were about her age. She describes her feelings in the following way:

> I was so angry and I am still angry. I felt I did not belong anywhere, neither in the institution nor at home with Dad. I am not angry at you or anyone specifically, I am just angry at having been made into a 'mentally retarded person'.

One way of surviving the institutional life was to pretend she was two different persons.

> Because I had to be there [in the institution] I decided not to be myself but someone else. I have two names and my first name is generally not used. I used that name for the girl in the institution. When I went home to Dad and my brothers and sisters every other weekend I could be myself and used my second name.

In her mind Ebba refused to belong to the life of the institution and the stigmatization that came with it. Her family was and still is the most important aspect of her life and she has always been very close to her father and her siblings. By pretending to be another person when she was in the institution she managed to find a way to survive the eight years she lived there and resist the stigma. Ebba refuses to accept the label of 'mental retardation' or 'learning difficulties'. She sees herself as physically impaired and is an active participant in an association for physically disabled people. Her strong resistance to the label of 'learning difficulties' derives from her experience that if you are seen as having learning disabilities 'people look at you as if you know nothing and can't do anything'.

Recent inclusive disability research, unlike Goffman's findings in *Stigma*, indicates that although society stigmatizes people this does not necessarily mean that these people share society's view (Goodley 2000; Walmsley and Johnson 2003) and in fact they may develop various ways of resisting the stigma. This was evident in the current research where the three women have actively resisted the stigmatizing label of learning difficulties and do not define themselves in those terms. Instead they think of themselves as an advocate, a pioneer, a poet and a working woman, and talk about themselves as sisters, cousins, daughters and wife. The women's self-image is therefore not confined to the label of learning difficulties. They are all conscious of their position as disabled but refuse to be defined solely in those terms. Ingiborg and Erla are proud to belong to a group of people with learning difficulties and are active self-advocates. However, the stigma of the label has had a profound and negative influence in their lives and all three have a great need to protest against it.

The importance of memories

Belonging and having roots constitute some of the most basic needs of mankind. Scholars point out that it is important for everyone to have relationships with other people, share mutual experiences and understandings of things. Everyone needs to experience that another human being understands their feelings and has faith in them (Goodley 2000; King, Brown and Smith 2003). The deepest roots of belonging most often lie in the family. Later in life other social relations are formed through various connections and people belong to different groups such as schoolmates, friends, co-workers, and so forth. The need to belong is strong and at the basis is the human need to strengthen their self-confidence and self-image (Ramcharan *et al.* 1997).

It is not difficult to imagine the effects of being sent to an institution as a child, far from one's family. The stories of the three women discussed here show that one way they coped with institutional life was to hold on to their memories of the years they had with their families when growing up and to keep in their thoughts the social relations they had with members of their families. This reflects their need to belong, be loved and understood. Holding the memories of being a part of a family and regular community life probably also helped them fight the stigmatization of being labelled 'different' from others and resist belonging to the life inside the institution. Their stories clearly indicate that the strength they sought in their childhood memories helped them resist and protest their situation.

Erla's story shows how exceedingly precious her memories of the childhood years at home were to help her survive the many years in the institution. Although she only lived with her family for two years as a child she described this time and her connections with her family in great detail many years later. For example, she has vivid memories of her father coming home from the sea, how each of his footsteps sounded as he climbed the stairs, how he smelled, the tone of his voice when he spoke with her and what he said. She describes how she often dreamed of being home again playing with her brothers and sisters and listening to her father tell them stories.

Ingiborg was nine when she was sent to the institution but has strong and detailed memories of her childhood years with her family. She describes, for example, how and what they ate:

> In the morning I always had oatmeal and sausage, and at noon fish and potatoes, and we drank water with the meal. For afternoon tea we had bread and drank milk and in the evening my mother often made soup and we had bread with it. It is not healthy to eat two hot meals a day.

Ingiborg often talks about all the things she missed out on and often asks her sisters and brothers what they were doing and where they had been after she was sent to the institution. These examples show a strong desire and need to belong to their families. The memories of the precious time of belonging were sources of comfort and reassurance of self-worth that gave the women strength to survive life in an institution and resist the situation they found themselves in.

Anger and sadness

A strong theme in the stories of Erla, Ebba and Ingiborg is anger and sadness but it was difficult for them to find acceptable outlets for these feelings. Ebba says:

> I was so sad and angry inside and if I wasn't angry then I cried, so it was better to be angry. I'm still angry and if I stop being angry then it seems to me that everything is all right. But it wasn't all right and a person should not forget it either.

Ingiborg expressed her frustrations and anger by hitting the staff if she felt that she wasn't treated well enough or when she did not feel well.

> I remember that I was so often angry while I was in the institution. I think it was because I wanted to be with my dad, my mother and brothers and sisters. Then I was never asked about anything. So I sometimes struck staff and then I was locked up, sometimes for a long time, sometimes for a shorter time. It was a difficult feeling to be locked up, I always feel best outside, being able to look at the flowers and then write a poem. I have composed poems every day since I was 18. I love looking at the flies and butterflies and honeybees and bees and wasps outside in nature, and spiders weaving their webs.

It is easy to imagine how the nature lover, Ingiborg, felt being locked up and having no control of the situation. Being out in nature and composing poems, Ingiborg managed to find a refuge outside the institution and thereby resisting and surviving the life inside.

Erla described how she was often angry and sad. She talked especially about the grief because of how much she missed her father. She dreamt about her life in her childhood home and tried to remember everything that had happened during the two years she lived with her family. It also made Erla sad and angry when the children and the more disabled people in the institution were treated badly. She tried to speak up for them.

When I became older I often looked after little children. I've always enjoyed being with children. Sometimes I think to myself that I would have liked to have taken one little baby that had no parents and raise it myself. In the institution everybody treated Baddi very badly. Once they threw him down the stairs. I said: 'What's wrong with you? Baddi can't help what he is like. You need to treat him nicely.' I tried always to look after him so that nobody could do anything to him.

Friendships and social relations

Holding on to memories of their families and their childhood back home was an important survival strategy for the women. Their stories also show the importance of friendships and other relationships they formed in the institution and after they moved out. Of the three women Erla lived the longest in institutions and had very limited time with her family. Her friendships from the institution became important aspects of her life. She said:

I had good friends in the institution and they often helped since I did not have a wheelchair. The boys made me a go-cart that they pushed me around in. Once my girlfriend took me picking berries. She carried me on her back and I put the berry pail around my neck and on we went and filled the pails with blueberries. It was a sunny day. Today my friend is a married woman who lives up north. I went to visit her last year and it was so much fun to see her. We talked and laughed all night long and talked about when we secretly made coffee late at night. You weren't allowed to drink coffee in the institution but Dad had sent me some.

The women's stories included a small number of stories of organized resistance. Most common were examples of the solidarity between those who lived in the institution. Some of the resistance was silent, but it was there in their minds and feelings of anger and sadness, which was difficult to express. There were, however, also a few signs of open protests and Ebba described with a bit of pride some of the ones she had taken part in. She recalled with great joy a play she and other residents at the institution had put on where they made fun of the staff. And there were other forms of protest:

Sometimes, if we had been bad, we got nothing to eat. Then we would steal food from the kitchen in the evening. We sneaked in and got something good for ourselves. It was fun and we laughed a lot. Sometimes I also ran away to Dad and got something to eat there. I was scolded when I got back. But it was worth it. I always felt I had won each time I did it.

Participating in self-advocacy groups has been important for the women. All were founding members of Átak (see above) and have been active self-advocates although Ebba later joined a different disabled people's association. Through the self-advocacy groups they established friendships and relationships with people with whom they share experiences and a common cause.

Ebba is the only one who is in a long-term relationship. She and her husband got married in 1993. She describes their relationship as a very good one.

I first met him when I slipped on ice and fell into his arms. I have been there ever since. We do everything together and although we do not always agree, that's all right, we are best friends. Since we got married I can always be myself and I know that he accepts me as I am and understands me. That makes all the difference. His family helps us and now I have two families.

The importance of telling one's story

Although not one of the intended goals of the life history group, participating in it has been an empowering experience for the women. Through telling their stories and being listened to they feel like they have received recognition for the difficulties they have had to endure. Erla, for example, often describes how much it means to her to have the opportunity to tell her story. Ebba, the pioneer, feels like her story is important and that others can learn from her:

Finally I get to say what I feel. Someone is listening to me. I've always wanted it that way... Finally everybody can see that I can do things and how I have felt. I can be myself. Then others can also learn from me. I have so much to say.

It has been argued that participation in an inclusive research group can be compared to people's participation in self-advocacy groups and that such experiences empower people to resist, stand up for their rights, speak up for themselves and be more independent (Goodley 2000; Walmsley and Johnson 2003). Ebba describes her experiences of being in the history group in such ways. Perhaps the most empowering experience for her was to travel abroad to an international conference where scholars and people with learning difficulties discussed research together. She told her story at the conference and met people from other countries who had experiences similar to hers. Participating in this conference was an extremely powerful experience for Ebba. Through this experience she saw her life as a part of a larger picture and gained a sense of common cause and belonging on a different scale than before. She is determined to continue working with people internationally on inclusive research.

During the first meetings of the history group both Erla and Ebba often cried when they recalled what happened during the years when they lived in the institutions. Eight months later they could laugh at some of these things. Talking about them and sharing them with others were powerful ways of healing and coping with these difficult memories. It has been a particularly powerful experience for the women to give presentations for university students who are training to work with people with learning difficulties. In these presentations the women tell about their lives and experiences and the roles have been reversed. Now, they have become the experts! Erla described how she feels about this new opportunity:

> Now I am a teacher and everybody listens to me. I am paid for it like everyone else. People who start working with people with learning difficulties have to listen to us. We can say how we feel. Staff shouldn't take their private lives with them to work and spend all their time talking about it. Then they are always talking about us like we are not there. I want to tell people who are training to work with us that I won't have it like that. This is our home.

Conclusion

This chapter has discussed the stories of three women with learning difficulties in order to learn lessons about resilience and resistance. The stereotype of women with learning difficulties is that of a passive victim. Their stories do not confirm this. Instead, the women's lives reflect active ways and strategies of coping with segregation and other difficulties. They were sent away from their families as children or teenagers to live under the all-powerful regime of the institution. The fear and loneliness of such an experience is hard to imagine. The most powerful way to survive this was holding on to the memories of belonging: being loved and cared for by their families. The memories of being a 'normal' person belonging to regular family life also gave them strength to resist the stigmatizing label of 'mental retardation' or 'learning difficulties'. All of them fought to hold on to their human dignity, independence and sense of self-worth. Their everyday strategies of surviving and resisting the institution varied. The poet, Ingiborg, found a means of escape in nature where she composed poetry about the beauty and freedom she found there. In her darkest times of despair, frustration and anger she hit the staff: that is perhaps the most openly expressed rebellion in the women's stories. The pioneer, Ebba, and other residents in the institution put on a play making fun of the staff. She and her friends also stole food when staff punished them by not giving them meals. Erla, the advocate, spoke up for herself and others despite running the risk of being punished and scolded for doing so.

Such acts as described above are rarely understood as acts of resistance or survival strategies. These are usually explained away as 'challenging behaviours' or the like. People with learning difficulties have historically been cast into many negative roles such as the role of the helpless eternal child or, even worse, as not human. It is therefore hard for many to relate to their common humanity and recognize their acts of resistance and resilience, even when it is openly expressed. Participating in the women's history group was an empowering experience for the women because it was the first time their stories of resistance and the hardship they survived was taken seriously and listened to. Telling their stories and having them heard has given the women a strong sense of being recognized and respected.

References

Atkinson, D. (1997) *An Auto/biographical Approach to Learning Disability Research.* Aldershot: Ashgate Publishing.

Atkinson, D. (2004) 'Research and empowerment: Involving people with learning difficulties in oral and life history research.' *Disability and Society,* 19 (7), 691–703.

Atkinson, D. and Walmsley, J. (1999) 'Using autobiographical approaches with people with learning difficulties.' *Disability and Society,* 21 (2), 203–16.

Atkinson, D., Jackson, M. and Walmsley, J. (1997) *Forgotten Lives: Exploring the History of Learning Disability.* Kidderminster: BILD.

Becker, H. (1963) *Outsiders: Studies in the Sociology of Deviance.* New York: The Free Press.

Bogdan, R. and Taylor, S.J. (1982) *Inside Out: The Social Meaning of Mental Retardation.* Toronto: University of Toronto Press.

Booth, T. and Booth, W. (1996) 'Sound of silence: Narrative research with inarticulate subjects.' *Disability and Society,* 11, 55–9.

Edgerton, R. (1967) *The Cloak of Competence.* Berkeley: University of California Press.

Goffman, E. (1961) *Asylums: Essays on the Social Situation of Mental Patients and Other Inmates.* New York: Anchor Books.

Goffman, E. (1963) *Stigma.* Boston, MA: Prentice-Hall.

Goodley, D. (2000) *Self-Advocacy in the Lives of People with Learning Difficulties: The Politics of Resilience.* Buckingham: Open University Press.

King, G., Brown, E. and Smith, L. (2003) *Resilience: Learning from People with Disabilities and the Turning Points in their Lives.* Westport, CT: Praeger.

Ramcharan, P., Roberts, G., Grant, G. and Borland, J. (1997) *Empowerment in Everyday Life.* London: Jessica Kingsley Publishers.

Rolph, S. (2002) *Reclaiming the Past.* Milton Keynes: The Open University.

Stalker, K. (1998) 'Some ethical and methodological issues in research with people with learning difficulties.' *Disability and Society*, 13, 1, 5–19.

Stefánsdóttir, G. (2004) 'Birtingamyndir andófs og mótspyrnu í lífssögum þriggja kvenna með þroskahömlun' ['Expressions of resistance in the life histories of three women with learning difficulties'], in Úlfar Hauksson (ed.) *Rannsóknir í félagsvísindum V [Social science research V]*. Reykjavík: University of Iceland Press.

Traustadóttir, R. and Johnson, K. (2000) *Women with Intellectual Disabilities: Finding a Place in the World*. London: Jessica Kingsley Publishers.

Walmsley, J. and Johnson, K. (2003) *Inclusive Research with People with Learning Disabilities*. London: Jessica Kingsley Publishers.

Ward, L. (ed.) (1998) *Advocacy and Empowerment*. Chorley: Lisieux Hall.

8

Songs of Resistance

Sue Ledger and Lindy Shufflebotham

People who lived in large institutions developed their own ways of resisting. Some of them did this through songs that they used to make up and sing. Some of the songs were about the nurses and some were about life on the wards or a better life outside. Some of them are funny and some are sad. Some show a great deal of anger. The songs were nearly lost because many of the people who lived in the institutions are getting old and dying. People with learning difficulties are no different from other groups of people who have used songs to help them to resist.

Introduction

This chapter will present a selection of songs composed and sung by people with learning disabilities whilst they were living in a range of segregated, long-stay hospitals and institutions. The songs clearly show that people with learning diffi-culties were speaking up for themselves, demonstrating resistance and resilience, long before the terms 'advocacy' and 'self-advocacy' came into common usage.

Bersani suggests that a social movement, such as the self advocacy movement, writes its own history and identifies its roots: 'A movement develops its own liter-ature and lore… It uses slogans and songs effectively to crystallize its agenda.' (Bersani 1998, p.65)

We argue that these songs, residual from the experience of living within institutions, represent an essential part of understanding the history of learning difficulty and therefore the history or roots of the advocacy movement. The songs not only provide evidence of resistance, they also tell us about important aspects of institutional life: the hierarchies, the rules, the sanctions, the work and the routines.

This chapter begins with a brief introduction about the methods employed to capture the material. After this we consider songs from five different institutions accompanied by brief contextual information on each setting. We conclude by discussing the importance of resistance songs to a variety of groups who have faced oppression.

The lost songs?

The songsters and songs recorded in this chapter have proved very difficult to trace. The Social History of Learning Disability group at the Open University had received reports of the existence of the songs for some time, yet following the resettlement of many people from the long-stay hospitals to a diverse range of community services many trails had gone cold. One of the authors personally knew several people who had lived at St Lawrence's Hospital, Caterham. These ex-residents were contacted and were able to confirm the existence of the songs but could not remember the words or the tunes. From these and similar interviews an increasing sense of urgency emerged for the need to trace and record this valuable source of material. There was a risk that the songs and music could be lost forever, as many of the older generation of former hospital patients were becoming increasingly frail.

Sadly, one of the former residents of St Lawrence's who knew many of the songs died shortly before the research for this chapter was undertaken. Her name was Sylvia Ironman and she had composed many of the songs herself. The following account by Anne Sage, the manager of the care home where Sylvia lived, demonstrates the detail of many of the songs but also the ease with which they have been lost.

> Sylvia moved to Surrey following her evacuation from central London during the Second World War and at the age of 14 went to live at St Lawrence's Hospital. Following resettlement from hospital and a brief period in London, in 1992 Sylvia came to live with us here, at the Conifers, a home for people with learning disabilities in Bridlington, Yorkshire. During her stay with us she frequently told us horror stories and many a sad tale about the

'mean' sisters and nurses that worked at the hospital and the length of time she spent there. The rhymes and songs we heard about St Lawrence's were very long and very detailed. Sylvia had many songs, poems and rhymes from her hospital days: phrases about the nurses and doctors which she would sing to herself and others. But St Lawrence's was in Surrey and Sylvia ended up living here in North Yorkshire so very little of it made any sense to us and although we all knew about Sylvia's songs we didn't think to write them down. Unfortunately we have no record of these songs and poems, only her more recent short rhymes. These are evidence of Sylvia's continued talent at composing rhymes residual from her days at St Lawrence's. Sylvia was a lovely lady and is sadly missed. We all have very fond memories of her. (Sage 2005)

Sylvia Ironman, who composed many of the songs from St Lawrence's

Following discussion with delegates at the Open University Testimonies of Resistance conference in 2001, a decision was made to try to trace the long-stay songs and songsters. The authors' informal networks were initially used to trace potential contributors and initially a sample of 250 people with learning difficulties and paid workers were approached. Additional potential sources were also contacted, including Values into Action, the Valuing People Support Team, People First organizations, a cross-section of service user groups and British Museum sound archivists. From a combination of all these sources the contributors in this chapter were identified. Visits were made to record songs on tape and these were subsequently transcribed. Two of the songs were extracted from memory books put together to commemorate hospital closures. Some contributors sent existing tapes accompanied by transcriptions. The song recordings we gathered were also played to contributors to generate further discussion and memories. The musical notation in this chapter was transcribed from our new recordings and existing recorded material.

Institutional life in five settings across the country provided the backdrop against which the following songs were recorded. For each setting we have included a brief context and in some cases we have been able to put this alongside the words of the contributors and their supporters. Additional context and music referencing has helpfully been provided by Roy Palmer, a music historian (Palmer 1988), and we have included these references in notes at the end of the chapter.

The Royal Albert Hospital, Lancaster

Admitting its first patients in December 1870, the Royal Albert Asylum in Lancaster received residents from the seven northern English counties. In the early years this voluntary institution focused upon the care and education of children and by 1909 it was home to 662 individuals. In line with the eugenicist spirit of the 1913 Mental Deficiency Act, with life long segregation in institutions increasingly viewed as the most appropriate way to respond to the needs of people with learning difficulties, the remit of the hospital changed to providing care for individuals of all ages and abilities. Rather than preparing its residents for integration with a wider world, the institution was now primarily concerned with segregation. In line with these developments the numbers continued to rise, so much so that during the 1960s and 1970s the hospital experienced serious overcrowding, with the patient population exceeding 1000.

This brief background however does not do justice to what life was actually like for residents. During the late 1980s, in Lancaster reminiscence groups of those who had experienced life as residents shared some of their memories (Ingham, Cowgill and Spencer 1987–9). Their personal hospital histories went back as far as the 1910s and covered a range of topics and themes including the daily routines, the work that patients had to do, stories of resistance and, much to the surprise of those working alongside the groups, the songs and rhymes of resistance. Unfortunately many of those who were present in those groups have since died, and so gathering more information on the exact context of these particular expressions of resistance has proved difficult. Nonetheless, they still provide an illuminating perspective on Royal Albert residential experience.

The Cocoa Song

'The Cocoa Song' is based on a Second World war song 'Gee, Ma, I wanna go home' much parodied in the Forces (see Palmer 1990, p.48). According to Stan Byers, a former Royal Albert resident, 'there was four of us what used to sing it. But I think there's only me knows it now.'

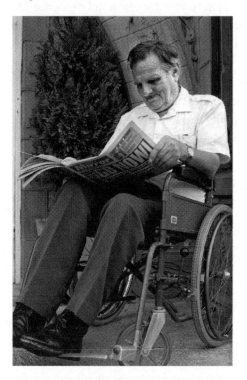

The late Stan Byers in 1990, outside his home in
Morecambe (photograph copyright © Helen Burrow)

The Cocoa Song
The cocoa that they gave us, they say is mighty fine.
It's good for cuts and bruises and tastes like iodine.
So I don't want no more of Royal Albert life.
Gee, Ma, I want to go home.

The stockings that they gave us, they say they're mighty sheer.
We put them on the clothes line and watch them disappear.
So I don't want no more of Royal Albert life.
Gee, Ma, I want to go home.

The bacon that they gave us, they say is mighty fine.
A leg fell off the table and killed a pal of mine.
So I don't want no more of Royal Albert life.
Gee, Ma, I want to go home.

The bacon that they gave us, they say is mighty fine.
The staff get the bacon, the patients get the rind.
So I don't want no more of Royal Albert life.
Gee, Ma, I want to go home.

The pullovers that they gave us, they say they're mighty fine.
One of Betty Grable's[1] will fit in two of mine.
So I don't want no more of Royal Albert life.
Gee, Ma, I want to go home.

The money that they gave us, they say is mighty fine.
They give us hundred shillings and take back ninety-nine.
So I don't want no more of Royal Albert life.
Gee, Ma, I want to go –
Gee, Ma, I want to go –
Gee, Ma, I want to go home.

Voice

The co-coa that they gave us, they say is might-y fine. It's good for cuts and bruis-es and tastes like i-o-dine. So I don't want no more of Roy-al Al-bert life. Gee, Ma, I want to go home.

Repeat for verse 2

Come to Barlow Song

Recorded by Stan Byers singing to the tune of 'Build a Bonfire'. Barlow Home was a Royal Albert ward opened in 1934 specifically for young boys, for whom it was their first experience of institutional life. The second verse of this song is a well known children's rhyme, sung to the tune of 'Clementine'.[2]

Come to Barlow Song

Come to Barlow.
Come to Barlow.
We will find it very nice.
If it wasn't for the nurses,
We would live in paradise.

Build a bonfire.
Build a bonfire.
Put the nurses on the top.
Put the charge hands in the middle
And we'll burn the bloomin' lot.

A hospital song

The following is a transcript of a recording of Peggy Palmer made during a Royal Albert reminiscence group.

> You can sing it about any hospitals though. I still know it though. This is the way they taught me at Leybourn Grange. They sing it like this though. I'll sing it about the Royal Albert though. This is the way they taught me. That's what they did teach me at Leybourn Grange.

This song also has military precedents during the Second World War; it is sung to the tune of 'Villikins and his Dinah'.[3]

Hospital Song

They say the Royal Albert's a wonderful place,
But the goings on there are a shocking disgrace.
The matrons and doctors have nothing to do,
'Cept stick their noses in the air when they're walking past you.

They say, 'Don't you worry, you'll soon be free.'
My worry is that they've strolled over me.
And I think it's useless to pull up your socks,
For when you go out, you shall go in your box.

Peggy died in 1994 and is fondly remembered by Jewli Winder, a nurse, who worked with her in the seven years preceding her death. During this time Peggy left the Royal Albert and moved into supported accommodation in the area. Jewli recalls that:

Peggy was a very proud lady; proud of how she conducted herself over the 'low grades' in the Royal Albert Hospital, she saw herself as far superior to everyone else, and loved to please staff and get praise for helping out around the wards… Her job at the Royal Albert Hospital was to make beds, which she did thoroughly and efficiently with her one good arm proficiently doing her 'hospital corners' on each bed. Peggy always used to say she would have been married with children if it wasn't for her 'paralysed arm and leg in a calliper' and used to say that's why her mum put her in the Royal Albert Hospital, and what a shame it was for her never having a beau (her wording). She loved her mum and family dearly…

After leaving the Royal Albert Hospital, Miss Peggy Palmer at her home in Lancaster (courtesy of Jewli Winder)

Jewli also recollects Peggy making:

fantastic rugs in the OT [occupational therapy] department at the Royal Albert Hospital and carried this over when she got resettled, making them to sell to family and friends. She had a little book that we used to record her 'business' in and how much she made for her rugs etc. I still have my rug in pride of place in my hallway. (Winder 2005)

Work rhyme

One man, who probably entered the hospital in the 1920s, recalled the following rhyme as a response to the hard work the residents were expected to do:[4]

God made the bees,
Bees made the honey,
The patients did the work,
While the staff get the money.

Royal Albert Song

This is a First World War song, recorded by Stan Byers during a Royal Albert reminiscence group. It is sung to the tune of 'What a friend we have in Jesus'.

Royal Albert Song

When I get my civvy clothes on,
No more soldiering for me.
You can tell the sergeant major
No more soldiering for me.

No more church parades on Sunday,
No more asking for a pass.
You can tell the sergeant major
To stick his passes up his arse!

St Lawrence's Hospital, Caterham

St Lawrence's was a large learning difficulty hospital situated on Caterham Downs. It was open from 1870 to 1994 and offered accommodation to well over 1000 people. St Lawrence's was arranged in 13, four-storey T-shaped blocks set out on two sides of an encampment of administrative buildings, workshops and other facilities: 'There is no escaping its penitential character' (Potts 2000, p.53).

The following songs and material were recorded during an interview with Doris Thorne in 2004. Doris was eager to emphasize how the songs and singing had played a very important part in maintaining her morale and spirit during some difficult times in hospital. Doris now lives in her own flat supported by staff whom she has helped to select and in whom she expresses a lot of confidence. She spent a large part of her early adult life as a patient at St Lawrence's Hospital. She was admitted at the age of 14 and eventually left at the age of 45. Doris has vivid recollections of frequent periods of solitary confinement in the padded cell, as punishment for what she herself describes as 'unruly behaviour' (Thorne forthcoming).

The hospital generated vast amounts of domestic work: miles of corridors and wards to clean and copious amounts of laundry to be washed and pressed. Whilst having a job was seen in some ways as a privilege, on other levels 'patients' were resentful at being forced to act as generally unpaid assistants to the nurses. The injustice of this was felt strongly. Not only were 'patients' required to do the work that nurses and others were employed and paid for, they were often required to work longer hours and were expected to do it with good grace and with far less remuneration.

In the hierarchical and authoritarian hospital regime Doris described how punishments were doled out to patients who questioned staff instructions or resisted their authority. Doris Thorne's response to the drudgery of the work, and the criticism she described receiving from staff, led to situations where she would answer back to the nurses, tear off her clothes in frustration and at times, when sufficiently upset, hit out at staff. This invariably led to periods of confinement in the padded rooms.

Doris Thorne's active, vocal and sometimes physical resistance to the nurses' use of authority was coupled with her conscious knowledge that the padded cell was not the worst form of punishment available. 'Patients' demonstrating physical aggression towards staff ran the risk of being sent to Rampton high security hospital. This was a place from which it was generally believed 'you only came out of dead' (Thorne forthcoming). People who lived in these institutions and resisted the machinations of the system lived with the day-to-day knowledge that worse punishments could be meted out by the staff. Fear of this acted as a further form of oppression.

These facts make the composing and singing of the songs all the more remarkable and risky. Doris Thorne used the songs as a way of both getting back at the system and relieving feelings of anger, frustration and helplessness. The songs acted as solace. Doris described composing her songs in the hospital's padded room as a way of making bearable the inhumane conditions to which she was subjected. The padded room involved the wearing of a 'ticking suit' which prevented movement of the arms. Doris gave a moving account of how one nurse ally risked the wrath of the hospital authorities by resisting the custodial duty of denying Doris access to cigarettes. This was achieved by the nurse sneaking Doris out of the ticking suit and the padded cell for a quick smoke. This same nurse also brought Doris additional and prohibited cups of tea. Doris attributes her release from this padded room on at least one occasion to this 'kind' nurse. This is a good example of nurses and 'patients' working together to resist the, at times, invasive, oppressive and inhumane conditions of the hospital regime. The nurse recognized Doris as a sentient and deserving human being just as Doris recognized the compassion and humanity of a nurse as caught up and confined within the system as she herself was.

Doris introduces the hospital song herself in this extract from her life story *Goodbye all the Nurses*:

> I used to work in the hospital laundry [late 1950s]. I used to iron shirts and the staff uniforms. I worked in the laundry for a very long time and I used to do the ironing for the staff what were in the hospital. And they put me on the ironing table, gave me an iron and an ironing board and asked me to 'Start now! And don't finish till I tell you to finish.'
>
> They put me in the padded cell and said 'You can stay there for 24 hours.' I hated it! I cried and cried! I wet on the mattress, I couldn't help it. And when it came to mealtime, they used to come to my padded cell and did bring my meals on a tin plate with a tin cup. And I had to eat with my fingers. I think that was disgusting! They just let me out to go to the toilet. I said 'I won't eat any of your rotten meal, it's vile! Keep it'... I was in the padded cells many times because of violence... I was always in trouble!
>
> I used to think up songs in the padded cell and sing them there... Here's one:
>
> At one o'clock in the morning
> I was dancing on the floor

Singing 'Mummy, Daddy, take me home
From this convalescent home!
I've been here for a year or two
Now I want to be with you'
Goodbye all the nurses!
Goodbye all the nurses!
Goodbye all the nurses!
And jolly good riddance to you!

(Thorne forthcoming)

Bradstow School, Broadstairs

Bradstow School is situated in the seaside town of Broadstairs in Kent. Despite its location the school is part of the educational services of London and used to be owned by the Inner London Educational Authority.

Bradstow was a boarding school for children labelled as having 'severe mental handicap'. The school provided residential accommodation for over 100 children and young people between the ages of 5 and 19. Many of the children sent to the school were from a diverse range of ethnic and cultural backgrounds and frequently found themselves living at considerable distance [90 miles] from their families and cultural communities.

Song from Bradstow

Susie Hayes, a former Bradstow pupil, remembers songs from her school days in the 1970s. The following is a song that Susie used to sing whilst at the school. The song is sung to the tune of 'I am a pretty little Dutch girl', also known as 'I had the scarlet fever'.[5]

Song from Bradstow
I had the German measles.
I had them very bad.
They wrapped me up in blankets
And threw me in the van.

The van was very bumpy, I nearly tumbled down
And when I got to Scotland
I heard the children shout,
'Mummy, Daddy, take me home

From this convalescent home.
I've been here six years or more,
Now they make me scrub the floor!'

Here comes Dr Allison
Sliding down the banister
'Oh good gracious,' says the nurse.
I'll tell Mum when I get home
The boys won't leave the girls alone,
They pull their hair and kick their legs.
I'll tell Mum when I get home.

Stoke Park Colony, Bristol

Stoke Park Colony was a group of institutions for people with learning difficulties situated near Bristol in the south-west of England. It was opened in 1909 'for the training and permanent care of the mentally defective'. The Stoke Park group was licenced to accommodate in the region of 2000 patients who were engaged in a range of activities, from laundry and baking to working in the gardens and helping on the childrens' wards. The last of this group of hospitals finally closed in 2000. Prior to closure former residents wrote a book of memoirs which included the Stoke Park Song. These memories were included in a section of the book entitled *Bad Times*.

If you shouted at anyone they gave you an injection, it made you feel drowsy.

They never told us what they were giving us. I got in the bath and couldn't get out. That was the tablet they gave me. I stayed in the bath all night, they just left me there.

I don't know how years ago they got away with it without getting caught. People don't believe you; they think you are telling a lot of lies.

They used to climb over the gate and run away. If you got caught you got put in a side room with one cup of cold water and one piece of dry bread and you had to be like that for a week or more.

As a punishment for the boys they used to roll a wet towel, put it in a knot and hit them across the back.

It's not like that now things have changed a lot since then.

We used to work in the south boot room. I used to clean shoes every night, after tea. We used to get a shilling a week. We used to sing our songs in the boot room, and when we used to hear the staff coming we used to stop because we didn't want them to hear us. They did get to hear us though.

(Stoke Park Hospital 1996, pp.13–14)

Stoke Park Song
This time next year, where shall we be?
Not in Stoke Park Colony
If I do, I'll play my tricks
Tear my nightshirt into bits

No more dirty cups of tea
No more cabbages full of slugs
No more treacle on our rice
No more skippies telling lies

Stallington Hall, Stoke on Trent

Stallington Hall was a long-stay hospital situated near Stoke on Trent. It officially opened on 10 May 1940 as 'a colony for mental defectives' and housed a wide age range from young children to adults. The institution provided accommodation, educational and social facilities for a total of 500 patients. The institution closed at the end of the twentieth century and *The Stallington Life Book* was published to record experiences of people who lived there (Gill, Williams and Newberry undated). The following reminiscence is taken from a section of this book entitled Happier Days:

> 'Stallington Hall, Stallington Hall, where I hate to be, the nurses always onto me.' We used to sing that and they used to shout 'Shurrup!' and we used to sing all the more.

Stallington Girls' Song
We are the girls of Stallington Hall
We work so hard each day
The roses that are in our cheeks
Will never fade away
They say that we are common
And common we will be
If it wasn't for the girls at Stallington Hall
Where would the nurses be?

Themes from the songs

When listening to the songs and hearing the stories told by people with learning difficulties, we noticed that a number of shared themes appeared to be emerging. These related to the content and purpose of songs across the various institutional settings where contributors had lived.

Isolation

Many people in the long-stay institutions felt very conscious that they were 'a long way from home'. People expressed feelings of abandonment and fear on arriving at the hospitals (Potts and Fido 1991). Such sentiments are echoed in several of the songs; for example, 'Mummy, Daddy, take me home' (Doris Thorne, Susan Hayes), 'I don't want no more of Royal Albert life' (Stan Byers). Many of the hospitals were situated in rural locations many miles from family, former friends and relatives. Transport for visits was often very difficult and visiting hours were also restricted by hospital rules.

Oppression and power differences

Many people felt they had been duped into being in the institution in the first place. The Barlow song introduces an ironic tone when it refers to the children's ward: 'Come to Barlow, Come to Barlow, we will find it very nice'. They had been promised something better only to find themselves having lost their liberty, often dependent on obtaining passes to leave the hospital buildings. They found they had limited access to education and were tied into working long hours for little if any remuneration, with hospital life stretching before them for an indefinite period. These fears are clearly articulated in Peggy Palmer's hospital song:

> They say, 'Don't you worry, you'll soon be free.'
> My worry is that they've strolled over me.
> And I think it's useless to pull up your socks,
> For when you go out, you shall go in your box.

Sadly for some residents this proved to be the case; many people were admitted when young, lived their lives and died in the institutions. Doris Thorne described how two of her siblings died at St Lawrence's (Thorne forthcoming).

There were no residents' committees or self-advocacy groups in the early hospital days and so no mechanism for formally expressing concerns. Residents were very conscious of the hospital hierarchies and several matrons were described by contributors as being very authoritarian. Stories were told of staff abusing power in a number of ways, for example the withholding of privileges, postponing family visits and assigning people menial, unpaid work. As discussed earlier, many residents were very conscious of the financial exploitation involved in the fact that they were working alongside nursing staff, caring for less able residents, or alongside maintenance or gardening staff, often working longer hours with no remuneration and the constant threat of punishment if complaints were made. People, however, were at pains to emphasize that amongst the staff there were often allies; these people frequently made a very strong and lasting impression and were spoken of very warmly.

Food

Food recurs as a theme in several of the songs. From Stoke Park and the 'No more dirty cups of tea' and 'cabbages full of slugs' to the Royal Albert 'cocoa' and 'bacon'. The food was often delivered to the ward on trolleys and was frequently of poor quality and served cold, so adding further degradation to the lifestyle experienced by many patients. Little attention was paid to the presentation and serving of food for people who needed soft or liquidized diets – the entire meal was frequently blended. Whilst some residents may have had access to the hospital shop, at mealtimes there was generally very little or no choice.

Humour / raising morale

Many of the songs served to poke fun at staff. 'Here comes Dr Allison sliding down the banister' in Susie Hayes's song and in the Royal Albert Hospital song, 'The matrons and doctors have nothing to do, / 'Cept stick their noses in the air when they're walking past you'. Such lyrics undermine the authority figures within the song. Humour is used as a vehicle for articulating disrespect in addition to serving as a valuable coping mechanism. The singing of 'work songs' together also seemed to raise morale when the patients were doing tedious jobs like cleaning the shoes at Stoke Park. Songs were also very important for Doris Thorne in her survival of solitary punishment. From the Stallington Girls' song we can see the lyrics flouting the authority of the nurses: 'Stallington Hall, Stallington Hall, where I hate to be.'

The patients' sometimes cynical observations of both the hospital regime and the staff, 'If it wasn't for the girls at Stallington Hall / Where would the nurses be?', reflect the acute insight many patients had into the pain of their surroundings and the situation in which they found themselves.

'Our songs – not for the staff'

The fact these songs have been difficult to unearth may reflect that the former practice of keeping the songs as discrete currency, within the learning difficulty community, has persisted. Many people interviewed, who could not remember the detail of the lyrics, referred to the existence of the songs and described the content as being 'naughty', 'secret', 'rude' and 'against the staff'. An ex-Stoke Park patient observed, 'We used to sing our songs in the boot room, and when we used to hear the staff coming we used to stop because we didn't want them to hear us' (Stoke Park Hospital 1996, p.14). Doris refers to making up her songs in the isolation of the padded room away from all the nursing staff. In a physical environment where people had very little personal space this private language may have been especially valuable.

People recalled occasions when these resistance songs were sung in from of staff. Stan Byers, for example, recollected singing the Cocoa song in front of hospital staff and residents and the impact it had on the hospital hierarchy:

> We had a concert at the Royal Albert and we sung it on the stage and two of the main persons walked out – that was Dr. Cunningham [Medical Superintendent] and Mrs. Wareing [Matron]. When they heard that they didn't stop any longer, they walked out.

Woven through many of the songs are the feelings of anger and resentment engendered by the grinding work regimes described by a number of the contributors. Doris Thorne describes her experience of the long shifts in the laundry, the Stallington Girls' song refers to the work done by the residents, and the work rhyme candidly expresses this sentiment in the lines 'The patients did the work/ While the staff get the money'.

The desire for a better life

Sometimes the deepest feelings can be expressed by the simplest language. Variations on the phrase 'I want to go home' are recurrent in many of the songs: 'This time next year, where shall we be? / Not in Stoke Park Colony'. Interestingly, themes of returning and going home also recur in slave music 'demonstrating a profound desire to reach heaven, where there is no rain, no tribulation and no slavery' (Silverman 1994). Although many people were admitted to the long-stay hospitals from difficult circumstances, people still yearned and planned for a better life outside.

Advocacy and songs

Shakespeare (1993) indicates that a major activity of the disability rights movement has been the development of a positive identity and group consciousness. There is much debate about the definition of a social movement amongst people with learning difficulties. Bersani (1998) suggests that social movements involve the emergence of a new dimension of identity, often drawing upon a characteristic formerly seen as a weakness. In the self-advocacy movement, as individuals who have grown up with the label of 'mental handicap' or 'mental handicap hospital patient' form their own organizations, begin to take on organizational and leadership roles and speak out to demand changes in treatment and policy, they are clearly going beyond the ascribed social role of 'mentally handicapped' or 'learning disabled'. In the past people were often depicted as passive objects of pity, as exemplified by the earlier Mencap society 'Little Stephen' logo, which was later challenged by the self-advocacy movement (Hersov 1996).

We would suggest the songs contained in this chapter offer increased understanding of the 'groundswell feelings' and experiences that fuelled the development, passion and growth of the learning difficulty movement in this country.

The importance of songs in the history of a movement

It could be argued that any social movement has a fundamental need for its members, and those it is seeking to influence, to understand its roots and history (Bersani 1998; Silverman 1994). This is as true of the history of self-advocacy as it is of the Black Civil Rights Movement and Women's Movement. However, as the old long-stay hospitals close and the generation who lived in them age and die there is a danger that younger people with learning difficulties coming up through the school systems and interested in joining the advocacy movement may not be aware of or may not see the relevance of earlier stories of resistance and struggle. It is hoped that collecting, circulating and publicizing songs such as the ones above may provide a vehicle for keeping alive the links between a critical part of learning difficulty history and today's advocacy movement.

Songs which give voice to the experiences of oppressed and disadvantaged groups and provide evidence of how people resisted are not, of course, limited to the lives of people with learning difficulties. The songs give valuable emphasis to the shared experiences linking people with learning difficulties to other groups who have faced different forms of oppression.

Jerry Silverman in the introduction to his 1994 collection of slave songs and music emphasized the power of such material and its current relevance for African Americans today.

> In these slave songs we hear the true voice of pre-Civil War black America. They evoke the heart and soul of the people who created them, here are the spirituals and work chants, the dirges of pain and loss, the bursts of rollicking humour and the hymns of hope and faith that belonged to America's enslaved men and women... A direct link between the captured Africans of centuries past and African Americans of today these songs offer Americans of all races an astonishing insight into their nation's history. (Silverman 1994)

Silverman goes on to consider how historical and contemporary social inequalities have obscured the major contribution of American Blacks to American culture. The historical reality of slavery and the combined racial isolation, segregation and sustained inferiority of the education provided to African Americans have had deleterious effects and in this respect we can see some parallels to the themes emerging from the learning difficulty movement. Isolation, segregation and lack of education are all issues that people with learning difficulties have experienced in terms of discrimination. People with learning difficulties, many of whom have experienced significant difficulties in communication, reading and writing, are certainly a group who historically have lacked access to conventional forms of media and formal routes of protest. Many people have lacked access to a vote and been unaware of the role of Members of Parliament and local government representatives.

Silverman considers that music provides a special insight into the persistent and inescapable social forces to which black Americans have been subjected. The excerpt below from Silverman's song collection is an example of such a legacy and the power of the images contained in such pieces.

Many Thousand Gone[6]
No more peck of corn for me,
No more, no more;
No more peck of corn for me,
Many thousand gone.

(Silverman 1994)

By including this excerpt of a slave song we are not inferring that the experiences and suffering endured by people enslaved in the American south are the same as the experiences of the many thousands of people with learning difficulties who lost their liberty through admission to the long-stay institutions. What we are seeking to do is highlight parallels of experience in terms of oppression and resistance that exist through the songs and oral tradition of other movements and link self-advocacy to other social movements (Bersani 1998).

Roy Palmer (1988) in his comprehensive anthology of songs and their social comment describes how balladry was once favoured as the vehicle for the views of a wide cross-section of people, but it increasingly became the voice of those who felt themselves to be excluded from other means of self-expression. Palmer points out that orthodox histories frequently represent only the establishment viewpoint whereas the songs give the, often missing, experience from a 'lived perspective'.

In a BBC radio broadcast transmitted in 2005, the playwright Arthur Miller described the recordings of protest songs which he made in the 1940s in Wilmington, North Carolina (Miller 2005). The black community that had built the area's shipyards subsequently experienced real hardship in obtaining work in the yards and protests ensued. Miller recorded the music inspired by this community's struggle for work alongside interviews with those composing and singing the songs. As we have found with the learning difficulty songs, Miller discovered that several of the songs were 'originals', made up by members of the community themselves on the picket line, whilst others were adapted from existing tunes and popular melodies of the time.

The limited song material we have to date would appear to confirm that these songs are a vital part of the history of learning difficulty. As the self-advocacy movement increases in age and strength it is important people know their history and the contribution that earlier resistance has made to changing things for the better. Angry or humorous, wishful or critical, fleeting or long remembered, these songs have the sound of history. As Silverman (1994) also points out in his analysis of slave songs, not only do resistance songs such as these represent a vital link to history they are also great fun to sing and play – enjoy them!

Notes

1   Betty Grable (1916–73) was an American actress whose films were popular during the 1940s and 1950s.

2.   See, for example, Frank Rutherford (coll.) (1971) *All the Way to Pennywell. Children's Rhymes of the North East.* Durham: University of Durham Institute of Education, p.42.

3.   One version of this song, known as 'The A25 Song', begins: 'They say in the Air Force a landings OK'. See Tawney (1987).

4.   Cf. traditional rhyme: 'God made the bees / The bees make the honey / The poor man does the work / And the rich man gets the money'.

5.   See Opie and Opie (1985, p.455). In the notes on this song the Opies also mention a version beginning 'Mother, mother, take me home / From this convalescent home' (p.456), which seems to be a version of the first Doris Thorne song.

6.   'On January 1 1893 President Abraham Lincoln signed the Emancipation Proclamation, which officially released all slaves from bondage in the South. As the word spread through the slave cabins, blacks began to move, slowly at first and then in ever-swelling numbers, away from the plantations and toward the Union armies. As they moved forward toward freedom, the people sang of those who had gone before them and of everything they were jubilantly leaving forever: the call, the lash, and the 'peck of corn' and 'pint of salt' slavery's rations.' (Silverman 1994)

References

Bersani, H. (1998) 'From social clubs to social movement: Landmarks in the development of the international self-advocacy movement', in L. Ward (ed.) *Innovations in Advocacy and Empowerment.* Chorley: Lisieux Hall.

Gill, G.P., Williams, J. and Newberry, S. (undated) *The Stallington Life Book.*

Hersov, J. (1996) 'The rise of self-advocacy in Britain.' In G. Dybwad and H. Bersani (eds) *New Voices: Self-advocacy by People with Disabilities.* Cambridge, MA: Brookline Books.

Ingham, N., Cowgill, S. and Spencer, D. (1987–9) Songs and rhymes recorded in reminiscence groups with former residents of the Royal Albert Hospital, Lancaster.

Miller, A. (2005) The Accidental Music Collector. Radio 4 broadcast.

Opie, I. and Opie, P. (1985) *The Singing Game.* Oxford: Oxford University Press.

Palmer, R. (1988) *The Sound of History.* Oxford: Oxford University Press.

Palmer, R. (1990) *'What a Lovely War': British Solders' Songs from the Boer War to the Present Day.* London: Michael Joseph.

Palmer, R. (2005) Personal communication.

Potts, M. and Fido, R. (1991) *A Fit Person to be Removed.* Plymouth: Northcote.

Potts, P. (2000) 'Concrete representations of a social category: consolidating and transforming public institutions for people classed as "defective".' In L. Brigham, D. Atkinson, M. Jackson, S. Rolph and J. Walmsley (eds) *Crossing Boundaries: Change and Continuity in the History of Learning Difficulty.* Kidderminster: BILD.

Sage, A. (2005) Personal communication.

Shakespeare, T. (1993) 'Disabled peoples' self-organisation: A new social movement?' *Disability, Handicap and Society,* 8, (3), 249–64.

Silverman, J. (1994) *Slave Songs.* New York: Chelsea House Publishers.

Stoke Park Hospital (1996) *Memories of Stoke Park Phoenix NHS Trust.* Bristol: Phoenix NHS Trust.

Tawney, C. (1987) *Grey Funnel Lines. Traditional Song and Verse of the Royal Navy, 1900–1970.* London: Routledge.

Thorne, D. (forthcoming) *Goodbye all the Nurses.*

Winder, J. (2005) Personal communication.

PART II

Speaking for Ourselves

Accounts of Self-advocacy in Action

9

My Life, My Choices

Paul Savage, Tina Wilkinson and Carl Worth

In December 1997 a group of people met in Sheffield to start a self-advocacy group for people with learning disabilities in Sheffield. It was decided that 'Speaking Up for Action' (SUFA) would be its name. We wanted to employ someone to work with us and after some training we chose our own worker. Self-advocacy is about speaking up for ourselves and helping each other to say what we want in our lives. One of our proudest achievements has been the Learning Disabilities Parliament. The parliament meets monthly and helps people in Sheffield and South Yorkshire to have a say about their own lives.

Introduction

This chapter describes the beginnings of a self-advocacy group and is an example of how people with learning difficulties have come together to organize resistance against poor attitudes and services and to campaign for people to be able to speak up for themselves.

What is Speaking Up for Action?

Speaking Up for Action is a self-advocacy group run by people with learning disabilities. We make the rules and decisions for our group. Self-advocacy is about speaking up for what we want. We think speaking up is important because sometimes people with learning disabilities are not treated the same as everyone else. We are not always given the same choices as everyone else and we are not allowed to make choices for ourselves. Sometimes we are not allowed to have our say or we are not listened to. Sometimes we are not treated with respect.

Some of the Speaking Up for Action group at SUFA's old premises

Speaking Up for Action is about speaking up for ourselves and helping each other to say what we want in our lives. It's about speaking up for our rights and for the rights of all people with learning disabilities. Speaking Up for Action is about having choices in our lives. We don't want to be told what to do. We want to know about a lot of things, then choose what we want for ourselves. We need good information to help us make the right choices. We want to make our own choices about jobs and where we live, about holidays, about relationships and about being ourselves.

Speaking Up for Action is about having the chance to show that we can live and work and be part of the community – the same as everyone else. We want to be important in our communities. We want to be treated the same as everyone else. We want to be treated as human beings. We want to be treated fairly. We want people to talk to us and we want people to listen to what we say. We do not want people to say or do things to us that we don't like. We are adults but sometimes people don't treat us like adults. We want to be given the chance to make mistakes and to take risks and do things our own way.

In the beginning

In December 1997 a group of people met at Voluntary Action Sheffield. It was a mixed group of people, some with a learning disability and some without. But they all had the same idea – to start a self-advocacy group for people with learning disabilities in Sheffield. This group would be independent of service providers. It was decided that 'Speaking Up for Action' would be its name. The steering group then talked with lots of people around the city to find out what people wanted and what ideas they had.

In May 1998 the group sent in a funding application to the council and the Care Trust. This was successful and it was decided that the project and the worker would be based at the Sheffield Citizen Advocacy offices. In October we had a huge party to launch Speaking Up for Action. During the first half of 1999 we had lots of training to help us choose our new worker. The first day of training started with a 'box of dreams' game so that we could start to think about the kind of person who could help us make our dreams come true. By the end of the training session we had decided what the person was going to do and what they should be like so that we could put an advert in the local newspaper.

The second training day was all about how we picked out the people we wanted to meet in person. This included an exercise called the 'Mystery of the Murdered Teddy' – we all had some detective work to do in solving the puzzle! We had to make decisions from the evidence we found. We used these skills when we looked at the application forms and in deciding who we would ask to come to an interview.

On the last day of training we practised skills in listening and remembering. We decided what questions we were going to ask at the interviews and we had practice interviews so that we could try out the scoring system.

Finally, after all this hard work, we interviewed and chose our new worker who started in September 1999. Since then we have gone from strength to strength. Over the years workers, members

Discussing important issues at the Learning Disabilities Parliament, or 'People's Parliament'

and volunteers have come and gone but the project has continued to grow bigger and stronger.

Jason and Carl meet with Debra Moore from the Valuing People team

What are we doing now?

The group continues to meet regularly to plan our work and we produce regular newsletters.

A lot of the work we do is about making sure that people who use services in Sheffield have a say in any changes that might happen. We also look at other projects and services to make sure they are doing what they are supposed to do. We train hospital staff, social workers and volunteers about what it is like to have a learning disability and about the changes that the White Paper *Valuing People* said should happen have happened. In fact, we are making sure that in Sheffield there will be nothing about us without us.

But one of our proudest achievements has been the Learning Disabilities Parliament. The parliament helps people in Sheffield and South Yorkshire have a say about important issues in their lives. The parliament meets monthly at the town hall. Groups from all over the region attend to talk about anything from getting a job, to person-centred planning and day services, to where to live. Not only people with a learning disability come to parliament – we have service providers, people from the Partnership Board and anyone else we think might be able to answer our questions and to tell us how they are improving their services. We use the information we get in lots of different ways: we write articles for our newsletter, we feed back to the Partnership Board and we go and visit people.

It's not all work, work, work though – we enjoy arranging social events and occasions for people to get together, like visiting London and hosting Christmas parties. We have visited Northern College regularly to gain new skills, like learning to be a management committee and running our own group.

Taking in sights of London in a rare relaxing moment

Chris looks after SUFA's stall on Information Day

The future

We are in an exciting place now, we are about to become an independent group. We are hoping to move into new premises soon. This will give us more room. We want to expand and work with more people, we want to become proper trainers and make our own money so that we can be truly independent. We want to be paid for the work we do – just like everyone else is. We want our place in history, we don't want to be forgotten. We want to still be here in ten years.

10

'What They Want – Yes, But What We Want – Bugger Us!'

Andy Docherty, Elizabeth Harkness, Malcolm Eardley, Louise Townson and Rohhss Chapman

This chapter is about the experiences of four people who are involved with People First in Carlisle. Andy Docherty explains that he no longer lets people walk over him and that he speaks up for his rights. Elizabeth Harkness says that disabled people should speak up for their rights and that education should mean lifelong learning. Malcolm Eardley works as the campaigns officer for Carlisle People First and he talks about the campaigns for transport that is easy for everyone to use and also for fire safety in day centres. Louise Townson explains that People First has given a lot of people the confidence and strength to move on if they are unhappy.

Introduction

People with learning difficulties have been treated badly over the years. This chapter is about our group members and what has happened in their lives. We think that self-advocacy has changed a lot of people's lives. It takes time for people to speak out and some people are frightened to and keep their feelings to themselves. But once you start you don't look back.

Some people are scared of change because they don't know what it means or how to go about it. We think it helps if you are involved in People First because then there are other people who can support you.

People First has helped many things to change. Twenty or thirty years ago the words 'learning difficulties' were dirty words. Some professionals used to tell parents, 'Put them in hospital and forget about them.' We think everybody with learning difficulties has such a lot to offer. Sometimes other people just focus on the negatives, of what people can't do, rather than what they can do. We think all people can live the same life and have just as fulfilled a life as anyone who has not got a learning difficulty.

Andy Docherty: 'Talking about the past can help people'

I am going to describe my life in hospital and how I moved to live in my own flat. I went to live in hospital at the age of five. Some of the memories I have when I was a child are good but some of the places I lived in were like a prison.

I used to miss my mother but she always wanted me to speak up. She said, 'What do you think you have a tongue in your head for?' In those days I was afraid to speak up because you didn't know what would happen to you, you might get punished. They wouldn't be allowed to get away with it these days; it would soon be stopped.

After hospital I moved away to live with relatives. I had a difficult time there and tried to move for a number of years. Each time my social worker would say, 'Try and talk to them, we must keep the family together.' He wouldn't listen to what I was going through. One day, after something bad happened, I decided I could never go back home. I told people at the adult training centre I wasn't going back, and that was it.

For a while I had to live in respite, miles away from my friends, but my friends at People First came to visit me and helped me get a new place. I've lived in my flat for ten years now and it's great. I've got a Direct Payment, which I manage, and I employ my own care staff. I found there were too many restrictions going through a care agency.

I think talking about the past can help people. People need to know what's happened, about our history, and speak up for their rights. I used to let people walk all over me but I won't let them now. People respect my position as Co-Chair of the National Forum, which I'm very pleased about. When I was younger, I didn't think I would see a day where I spoke up for myself. If my mother could see me now she would say to herself, 'I don't believe it!'

Andy Docherty

Elizabeth Harkness: 'Too many people have been written off'

I think disabled people should speak up for their rights and that education should mean lifelong learning. Too many people have been written off. People may start school at three years old and at the moment state education stops at 19 years old. But I believe people with learning difficulties should be able to go on to university. I am finding out about how to do a Ph.D. I have been advised to ask about further education to get more qualifications.

I didn't used to speak up for myself but now I say to other people that they should all learn to speak up for themselves and join a group. People don't speak up because they are scared of what's going to happen to them. People should be able to make their own choices and get the right support they need.

Elizabeth Harkness

Malcolm Eardley: 'I'm going to turn it all around'

I worked as the campaigns officer for Carlisle People First. We have been working on an anti-bullying campaign – about how people with learning difficulties get bullied and abused by other people and what you can do about it. There has also been a campaign on decision-making about how people with learning difficulties don't have the same rights as everybody else in law. This is wrong. We also campaign about transport and making sure it is more accessible for people. We have also looked at fire safety in day centres for people with learning difficulties.

There are a lot of things that are wrong and need to be changed. That is my job. When I got to People First I said I'm going to turn things around and get things organized. I'm on a lot of groups to talk about people with learning difficulties like the local voluntary services and Mencap.

Malcolm Eardley

Sometimes things are difficult for people. It's happening all over the world and it needs to stop. It's bad when things go wrong and break apart and you don't know what's happening. Professional people should know that they have destroyed people's lives and they should do something about it. People with learning difficulties need to know what is happening and if they don't like it they should change it. That is what People First is about.

Louise Townson: 'People's lives have been wasted and it's an absolute discrace'

I was born in Carlisle but moved away to a special school in Newcastle when I was only four. Obviously I was distressed as I used to spend half the week away at school until the Wednesday. After a year I had to stay there all week. When I was 12 I moved to a school in Liverpool run by nuns who were very strict.

I went for my further education in Birmingham. Although it was hard for me and my family, being away from home, it was actually the best thing. I feel I benefited from the education I had rather than going to a larger, mainstream school. I have been shocked at finding out about the lack of education opportunities a lot of people with learning difficulties have had. I'm quite appalled that people I know were just given bricks or sand to play with and told they would never be able to do things. It seems like they were in a nursery school for the whole of their schooling.

I joined People First in February 1993 by attending the evening meetings. I was invited by a friend who was already a member. In 1994 the group gained some funding and we moved into our first office, which was very small. Later I started to work at the office doing secretarial work. Since then I have become the administrator for Carlisle People First and now I am the project director.

The way we work is that we're all good friends rather than just a group of people. We actually support each other through difficult things. I'm not saying that everyone in the group agrees all the time and we do have times when we disagree. This enables us to have good discussions. These discussions may get heated but once it's sorted out we move on to the next thing because there are bigger fish to fry.

I have been on a lot of different groups like the Government Taskforce and the National Forum.

Through the years I have seen some awful situations people with learning difficulties have been through, especially people who lived in institutions. For example, women being put into an institution because they had a baby outside marriage or society thought they were 'moral defectives'. The mothers were put away for 50 or 60 years and never saw their babies again. Some of them, when they left the institution, died because of the stress of the change. It upsets me to know people have been treated this way because it is criminal. People's lives have been wasted and it's an absolute disgrace.

Louise Townson

Since I've been at People First I've met a lot of different people. It's opened my eyes and I think it has given a lot of people the confidence and the strength to move on if they are unhappy. I really think that being in People First has helped me personally through quite a lot of things in my life since I became involved 11 years ago.

11

The Life of a Group and a Personal Story

Experiences from Huddersfield People First

Jeremy Hoy, Dries Cautrels and Dan Goodley with Huddersfield People First

Huddersfield People First started in 1986. It is a self-advocacy group for people with the label of learning difficulties. We meet every month to talk about our news and views. We speak up for ourselves and our rights. We raise money to fund the group and we are independent from services. We have been to conferences in Wales, Scotland, Canada and England. Self-advocacy is about learning from each other, making our own decisions and taking control of our lives. Jeremy Hoy is a member of the group and he tells us how the group works and how different people do different jobs and that everyone helps each other.

Introduction

This chapter is split into two sections. The first, reflections on Huddersfield People First, presents an overview of our group that we presented at the 'Testimonies of Resistance' conference at the Open University. The second, one story from the movement, draws on a project undertaken by Jeremy Hoy (transport officer and co-secretary of Huddersfield People First) and Dries Cautrels (a researcher and coach to the Belgian self-advocacy group, Onze Nieuwe Toekomst). They worked together to write Jeremy's story in late 2003. At a meeting in October 2004, members of Huddersfield People First agreed that the group's adviser Dan Goodley should put the two pieces of research together and add illustrations, an introduction and a conclusion for this chapter.

Reflections on Huddersfield People First

Members wanted to give their thoughts on being in a group. Here are just some of their reflections.

How long has the group been going?

We started in August 1986. A number of our members, including Khadam Hussain, Winifred Joyce and Joyce Kershaw, had heard about People First groups from staff in the day centre. Huddersfield People First was set up and we originally met in the Co-op – away from the day centre. In 1991, we moved our meetings to St George's Square in Huddersfield. Currently, we are in the meeting rooms of Voluntary Action Kirklees in Lord Street.

What is Huddersfield People First all about?

Huddersfield People First is a self-advocacy group for people who have the label of 'learning difficulties'. We meet monthly to talk about our news and views. We speak up for ourselves and our rights.

Huddersfield People First member Christine Abbott pictured with young friend

Members of the group discuss 'news and views'

We raise money to fund the group through activities such as sponsored walks and swims. We are independent from services. We go to conferences to meet other People First groups. We have been to conferences in Wales, Scotland, Canada and England. Self-advocacy is not just about being in a group but about learning from each other, making our own decisions and taking control of our lives.

Conferences that we have been to

In 1986 a number of our founding members attended the first British-based International People First Conference in Twickenham. In 1993, a number of our members attended the International People First Conference in Canada. On 19–22 September 1994 we went to the UK People First conference held at the University of Bangor, North Wales. In 1997, five members of the group attended the national People First Conference held in Edinburgh by People First Scotland. We have also been involved in discussions about setting up an England People First.

Khadam Hussain, Treasurer

One story from the movement

Jeremy, 34, is one of the 'hard-core members' of Huddersfield People First. He lives in Skelmanthorpe, Huddersfield, with his parents. 'I really like Huddersfield.' He is very active in the organization, being responsible for some important tasks, like helping people. Every decision is taken by the whole group by voting. 'If someone comes, we first have to discuss if they can come.' Jeremy is also an employee at Huddersfield's local newspaper, *The Examiner*.

To Jeremy, self-advocacy is a case of becoming stronger and making decisions on your own. Taking care of each other also seems very important to Jeremy.

Jeremy' Hoy

Jeremy's story

I work every morning at *The Examiner*: I deliver the mail. I also do the recycling. I get paid for this job, which is important to me. It really means I've got work. If we have an event, the group asks me to get it in *The Examiner*. They then usually send a photographer.

A copy of The Huddersfield Daily Examiner

To me, self-advocacy means helping people. Some people in our group can't read, so we need somebody who can. We are very helpful. We also have our letter meetings, together with Wendy Booth, our other adviser. Wendy is one of the two advisers of Huddersfield People First. The other people of the group are all right, I like them. We have always had good relations at People First. With Christmas, we go out for a drink. We go to the nearest pub, 'cause there are some people who can't walk far. When we have a new member, we meet at the bus station. I then take him or her down to the meeting. Then we discuss what we do and get them settled in.

'I'm proud of being a member of People First Huddersfield'

I joined People First Huddersfield to see and meet new people, and tell them what I think of People First. We also like to learn and get to know new people. I like meeting people and go to different groups around England. Sometimes they have conferences and invite us to talk about what we do. Therefore we do fundraising. We have a treasurer who is responsible for that. We also look at the future. We like helping other groups.

Self-advocacy also means sticking up for ourselves. We don't like being picked on. That is a message to other people. Being a member of our People First group also means speaking up for yourself. Nobody should tell me what to do. Self-advocacy is important to me.

No-one has the right to pick on us. If someone picks on me, then I just ignore them. We like being *people* first. We want other people to look at us just as normal people. And we want everybody to treat us like normal people. Sadly enough, that's not always the case. When I experience that I am really being picked on, or when other people are being picked on, I just go to the advisers or the police. Or have a word with the person who does this.

We have the same rights. But I feel all right, I don't experience too many difficulties. I think the self-advocacy groups make people a little aware. We have the same rights as everybody.

We like being called people with 'learning difficulties'. That's what we are called and that's what we are. We changed the term 'learning disabilities' – we didn't like that. We like our expression more, 'cause we chose it ourselves.

Jeremy outside the train station in Huddersfield

Going to People First, I feel stronger. Other people also become stronger. It means speaking up for yourself.

I like going out. Travelling around and meeting people. I like travelling on my own. I go anywhere, to Leeds for instance. And then I get on another bus and just go somewhere else. I like going out early, so I can be back early.

Jeremy likes to tell other people about Huddersfield People First

We like meeting and discussing things. We have 'News and Views'. We then go round the table, and if anybody has any news or a problem, they can say it. We then talk about it and try to sort it out. If we have any difficulties, we talk about them, and then we help and advise each other. You can also learn stuff, like what other people do. Going to the meeting is interesting.

We have someone who does the agenda, and I pick the letters up. We put pictures on it, so we know what we're looking at. 'Cause it's easier if we have pictures on. The advisers help us out. If we have a meeting and Danny isn't there, we manage it on our own. We can cope on our own without an adviser too. Danny needs to write things down. But we are in charge and we do it on our own; we have a chairman. If we have anything to say, we have a say.

We've been going a long time. We used to meet at the Co-op, where we had a big room upstairs. Then we moved down to Railway Street. And then we moved to Lord Street. That's where we've been ever since. Now we are looking for new members. We have leaflets that we give out.

Conclusion

This chapter has given some insight into the self-advocacy movement through the reflections of a group and the story of one of the members. The historical documentation of self-advocacy has never been more timely. New government legislation has pushed for the setting up of partnership boards and the funding of self-advocacy groups by the Department of Health. In the midst of such changes we can often overlook those pioneers who helped to establish a climate in which self-advocacy groups could grow and grow. It is safe to say that without the established People First groups in this country, policymakers would not have been so readily supportive of self-advocacy over the last ten years. Too often, formal histories of user involvement and disability politics tend to celebrate key policy initiatives and radical service providers – rather than resistant disabled people. We hope that this chapter goes some way to add to the testimonies of resistance presented in this book.

PART III

Alliances with Others

12

Fires Burning

Advocacy, Camping and Children with Learning Disabilities in Ontario, 1950–1990

Jessa Chupik

Jessa Chupik traces the history of the way in which the summer camping movement for people with disabilities has developed in a part of Canada. It has been difficult for people to decide whether young people with learning disabilities should have their own summer camps or join in with the ones set up for young people without disabilities. Jessa writes of how people with learning disabilities have been discriminated against and how some families have resisted this.

Introduction

In the early 1990s, an employee from the Saskatchewan Association for Community Living, a Canada-wide organization whose goal is to promote and advocate for inclusive environments for people with learning difficulties, was giving a presentation about community living to young children at a school. She started the presentation by asking the children what they thought that 'community living' meant. In her experience, she felt that it was important to try to define the meaning of the association to adults and children alike. After a few moments, a young girl who was six years old happily explained:

> I think community living is when you live on your block and go to school, or if you're big you can go to work, and if you're a kid you can go to swimming lesson and Brownies or Girl Guides when you're bigger and you can go to the store with your mom and dad and you can go to McDonald's and when you're older, you can drive a car and go to McDonald's yourself 'cause you have your own money, and you have friends to play with on your street and maybe you have a paper route and you can go to the library and walk your dog or go to birthday parties like I did on Saturday and have sleepovers and you know people when you walk down the street and people wave at you and say hello because they know you and you say hello back because that's how to be a friend. I think that's what community living means. Right? (Schwier 1991, p.23)

This little girl's definition includes many elements that illustrate what community living means to people with learning disabilities and their families who have struggled for access to community involvement. Although it was quite simple for this child to define, it has been much more complex for self-advocates and advocates to achieve. In Ontario there has been significant societal resistance to allowing a child with learning difficulties to attend swimming lessons or to join Brownies. It has been difficult to meet the overarching rhetoric of community living, largely due to the resistance faced by advocates in accessing mainstream organizations. Discrimination has run deeply and this chapter will, by using the example of camping, demonstrate the depths of inequity that has been faced by advocates and self-advocates in Ontario.

Going to summer camp is an important part of culture for a large minority of Ontarians. Camps exist across Canada, but the majority are located in Ontario (Hodgins and Dodge 1992). Although attending camp is largely a middle-class activity and not available to all young people in Ontario, the activity is so culturally significant that it has become important to gain access for people with learning difficulties. The fight for access for people with learning difficulties to summer camps provides an example of resistance to ingrained societal discrimination. The struggle encapsulates the contradictions of community living programming and the segregated camps run by the association. Advocates fought for access to both private camps and integrated environments. Although segregated summer camps were developed, these were a temporary solution that quickly became meaningful for children and families.

Advocacy in Ontario

Initially, the advocates for young people with learning difficulties to attend summer camps were parents who began to campaign in the 1940s. During this time there was a continued rise in the number of people admitted to the large institutional settings across the province of Ontario. The scale of the institutional setting was such that it was not until the late 1970s when the number of people who were able to access community-based programmes surpassed those living in institutional settings run by the government. A group of parents in Kirkland Lake, a small northern community, felt strongly that they wanted their children to be educated in their communities rather than be placed in institutions. Discussions with their local school board resulted in auxiliary classes for their children. This was initially restricted to children with an IQ of more than 50 and the parents campaigned for funds to extend the service to children with an IQ of less than 50. This initial success in Kirkland Lake encouraged others to start similar campaigns and by 1950 an advocacy group had been formed for the whole of the province of Ontario known as the 'Ontario Association for the Mentally Retarded'. This organization kept its name until the 1970s, by which time the People First movement had begun in Ontario and there was pressure on the association to change its name to the 'Ontario Association for Community Living'. Under this name the association has become one of the most influential advocacy groups in Canada. A history of the association was written by Betty Anglin and June Braaten partly to celebrate its silver jubilee in 1975 (Anglin and Braaten 1975).

The beginnings of the summer programmes

The early official documents of the organization demonstrate key areas of advocacy, including education, the closure of institutions, community-based programmes and access to recreation and camping programmes. The social class of advocates had some impact on the different goals of advocacy since the economic strain of caring for a child with learning difficulties was draining and therefore many parents felt that access for their child to recreation and camping was unachievable, as even if it were encouraged they would not be able to afford the fees that were required. However, in the 1940s and 1950s such opportunities were virtually non-existent because most people seemed to think that children with learning difficulties could not benefit from them. In order to combat this view, members of the association started three pilot projects during the 1950s. These included programmes for a summer playground, swimming and a square dance group. These projects were extremely successful and encouraged advocates to start similar programmes and recreational committees in their own communities.

The first segregated camp for children with learning difficulties started in 1956 at the Guelph Kiwanis Camp Belwood. The following year the director of the camp asked the association if they would take over its management so that they could provide a full programme for the children. June Braaten became the programme director and in the absence of a clear model to follow she adopted an experimental approach. 'Neither I nor my counsellors knew what retarded children could do so we tried everything' (Anglin and Braaten 1975, p.18).

Camp Belwood was considered to be a great success and it led to a number of new segregated summer camps for children across Ontario in the 1960s. Because of Ontario's vast size, it was felt that local associations should try to open their own camps and thus relieve the large numbers of children kept on waiting lists to attend Camp Belwood. Nine other regions began to operate camps and by 1965 over 1000 campers were singing the common opening song, 'Fires burning', around campfires (Anglin and Braaten 1975, p.41).

Attempts to integrate

Advocates saw the segregated camps as a staging post to the eventual goal of the inclusion of children with learning difficulties into the existing camp system. It was felt that when others saw the potential of the children in the segregated camps then this would change public opinion. Unfortunately, this process was very slow and many children and families became dependent on the segregated camps.

The Lakehead Association for Community Living in the northern community of Thunder Bay provides an excellent example of this dependence and of the methods of advocates. In the late 1960s the association, according to its annual reports, established a summer camping programme in order to meet the need for a leisure programme for its clients (LACL undated). The number of children able to attend the camp was limited by a lack of appropriate staff to work at the camp and also a lack of funds to buy supplies for the activities. In the early 1970s only about 40 campers were able to attend (LAMR 1972).

The advocates developed creative solutions for the shortage of money. It was cheaper for example to camp in provincial parks rather than to rent summer cottages or a children's summer camp. In 1977 over 70 campers attended 'Tenting 1977' at a local provincial park. This was considered to be a great success as children and adults with learning difficulties had the opportunity to meet and interact with others (LAMR 1977).

The debate about integration seemed to come to a head in 1979. The chairperson of the Leisure Services Committee wrote the following in her annual report:

> May I ask those same parents to investigate the advisability of placing their young people in a segregated program. Please try to steer them towards an integrated program. Let's be very realistic about what we want for our people; I am not asking you to do anything different for your handicapped child than you would do for the other children in your family. If we expect our young people to give us their best, then that is exactly what we will receive. (LAMR 1979)

There was some progress in accessing recreational programmes (more significantly than camps) for people with learning difficulties but it was still inadequate. Out of 500 people accessing other programmes through the association in 1980, only 75 of them were able to have some meaningful leisure activities (LAMR 1980). It was not until 1988 that the camps organized by the Lakehead Association were physically integrated into a mainstream camp environment (LACL 1988). Up until this point, camps were held at various available sites segregated from other camps and children. Holding the camps in a physically integrated setting was a great success for the association. However, physical integration did not always lead to social integration and this has remained a challenge in northern communities.

Integration – a continuing struggle

The experience of the Lakehead Association points to a number of key issues that had to be faced from the 1960s to the 1980s. Was it more effective to organize a segregated camp for people with learning difficulties, should there be integration or should the association put its efforts into day camp environments? Other associations across the province were also struggling with this question. The response from the government of Ontario was to fund an experimental programme in the summer of 1975 to find out what kind of experiences were most meaningful to people with learning difficulties.

The programme consisted of four different types of camps. The first was an adult work camp where 16 residents prepared the camp site and were paid minimum wages. Staff ran recreational activities, but it was made clear that staff worked for the campers. Campers appointed one individual from each cabin to represent them at the camp committee to ensure that their needs were being met appropriately. The second camp was integrated and eight campers who lived in an institution and eight other campers of a similar age (10–14 years) were integrated. The third camp was for juniors aged between 10 and 14; the purpose of this segregated camp was to prepare children with learning difficulties for the skills that they would need in an integrated environment. Finally, the fourth camp was a segregated recreational camp for young people aged between 18 and 24. Camp skills were emphasized and a four-day canoe trip was included. The philosophy of each two-week camp was to promote individual growth and to encourage self-motivation. The results of the experiment were published in the journal of the Canadian Association for the Mentally Retarded (Bumstead 1976).

The results indicated that it was the integrated camp that was the most successful. Researchers and campers alike discovered that social acceptance between campers developed within a few days. When problems arose, staff members were able to provide good support to the campers and sidelined any major issues. In the other camps the most meaningful components were the trips out. During these trips, campers developed self-understanding and personal growth, as measured by the researchers. The recommendations from the study included making clear that integration was the goal for camping programmes and that this should be much more than tolerance. There should also be ongoing preparatory camping programmes for individuals, and low-ratio integrated camps (Bumstead 1976). The mainstream camps for the most part did not heed these recommendations. For example, from 1975 to 1977, of the 168 camps approved by the Ontario Camping Association, only four were accessible to children with learning difficulties (Canadian Camping Association 1975, 1976, 1977).

In their campaign to promote integration, advocates faced a range of difficulties. While on the surface regular camps were receptive to integration, they were challenged by lack of financial resources and lack of time (and sometimes lack of commitment) to train young teenage staff to foster integration. As a result segregated settings continued. Furthermore, due to the lack of resources at the association, adults with learning difficulties were being placed in settings that were not age appropriate. This included occasions when adult campers were being directed by teenage counsellors.

Negative attitudes persist

Unfortunately, far from counteracting negative attitudes and acting as a staging post to integration, segregated or age-inappropriate camp projects sometimes had the effect of reinforcing stereotypes. An American example demonstrates this problem. One of the counsellors who had been working at a religious camp for people with learning difficulties wrote an article that was published in the largest camping magazine in the United States and widely distributed in Canada. The author, meaning to reflect on her experiences in overcoming discrimination through her religious beliefs, entitled her article 'To love ugliness'. This was a rare moment to challenge stereotypes but unfortunately the author wrote:

> As I looked around the room, I was repulsed by their adult bodies which harboured childish minds. How would I make it through the camp was a mystery... I knew I had to stay at camp with these 70 creatures. There was no way out...

Furthermore, as the week progressed, her attitude remained offensive:

> My cabin became decorated with crafts which my girls [note: these are adult women] made. Although many times my three year old sister could have done better, I saw a certain beauty in those finger paintings. (Ziegler 1974, p.12)

It was only, Ziegler claimed, through the strength of her religion that she was able to survive the week. This young woman unintentionally demonstrated that such deeply ingrained stereotypes about people with learning difficulties, especially about their childlike nature, were being perpetuated by sending adults to a children's camp.

Whilst camps slowly reacted to the need for accessibility for young people with physical disabilities, those with learning difficulties continued to be rejected for registration on grounds such as lack of specialist staff or lack of experience of camping. Furthermore, if these problems could be overcome an additional barrier for parents was the one of cost: segregated camps were often less expensive than the integrated ones.

Tensions continue

This chapter has concentrated on the resistance of many parents to the situation in which they and their children found themselves in from the 1940s onwards. Unfortunately, the tensions have continued and have become part of a wider debate between segregation and integration of services for people with learning difficulties. Although integration may be the goal for many advocates, people have become very attached to the segregated camps that have been set up across the province of Ontario. Indeed there has been an overwhelmingly negative response to the closing of two Easter Seals segregated camps at the beginning of the twenty-first century (Henderson 2002). Such camps have clearly provided a service for many young people with learning difficulties and their families. Whilst there remains a tension between segregation and integration it is clear that without the resistance of parents in the first place there would be no summer camp facilities at all. Attachment to and the cultural significance of segregated camps is described in a letter published by the *Toronto Star* by a former Easter Seals camper, Christine Ladner:

> In order to be accepted by their peers, many disabled children and teenagers feel the need to prove to their peers that they are bright and capable enough to be given equal opportunities. This can be an exhausting and frustrating task. It was during my first summer at camp that I realised it was ok just to be me. (Ladner 2002, A27)

References

Anglin, B. and Braaten, J. (1975) *Twenty-Five Years of Growing Together: A History of the Ontario Association for the Mentally Retarded.* Toronto: Canadian Association for the Mentally Retarded.

Bumstead, T.K. (1976) 'Experimental camping.' *Mental Retardation/Deficinece Mentale,* 26 (2), 7–10.

Canadian Camping Association (1975) National Directory Issue. *Canadian Camping.* Edmonton, Alberta: Canadian Camping Association/ L'association des camps du Canada.

Canadian Camping Association (1976) National Directory Issue. *Canadian Camping.* Edmonton, Alberta: Canadian Camping Association/L'association des camps du Canada.

Canadian Camping Association (1977) National Directory Issue. *Canadian Camping.* Edmonton, Alberta: Canadian Camping Association/L'association des camps du Canada.

Henderson, H. (2002) 'Mother decries move to close special camps: Easter Seals can't meet the needs of 110 children.' *The Toronto Star,* January 29, A04.

Hodgins, B. and Dodge, B. (eds) (1992) *Using Wilderness: Essays on the Evolution of Youth Camping in Ontario.* Peterborough: Frost Centre for Canadian Heritage and Development Studies.

LACL (1988) *Annual Report of the Leisure Services Committee.* Thunder Bay, Ontario: Lakehead Association for Community Living.

LACL (undated) *LACL Vacation and Leisure Opportunities – Staff Manual.* Thunder Bay, Ontario: Lakehead Association for Community Living.

Ladner, C. (2002) 'For many disabled kids, camps were a magical place.' *The Toronto Star,* May 7, A27.

LAMR (1972) *Annual Report.* Thunder Bay, Ontario: Lakehead Association for the Mentally Retarded.

LAMR (1977) *Annual Report.* Thunder Bay, Ontario: Lakehead Association for the Mentally Retarded.

LAMR (1979) *Annual Report*. Thunder Bay, Ontario: Lakehead Association for the Mentally Retarded.

LAMR (1980) *Annual Report*. Thunder Bay, Ontario: Lakehead Association for the Mentally Retarded.

Schwier, K.M. (1991) 'Understanding is child's play.' *Entourage*, winter, 23.

Ziegler, V. (1974) 'To love ugliness.' *Camping Magazine*, January, 12.

13

Resistance in Mencap's History

Liz Tilley

Mencap was started in 1946 as a group that fought for better services and support for people with learning difficulties and their families. It has always been involved as part of the resistance against poor services. It has fought against many of the bad attitudes towards people with learning difficulties. However, some people, such as self-advocates, researchers and parents, have argued that Mencap has been partly to blame for these bad attitudes towards people with learning difficulties. Several times since 1946 Mencap has had to change to make sure that it has kept up with different views.

Introduction

Mencap is a national organization that works for and with people with learning difficulties. From its founding in 1946, it has grown to become the largest voluntary organization concerned with learning disability in the UK, with over 15,000 members and 1000 affiliated groups. Resistance has been a key theme running throughout Mencap's history, but the forms that it has taken over the course of the past 60 years have been varied, complex and, at times, paradoxical. Throughout its history, Mencap has actively resisted society's prejudices towards people with learning difficulties. In repositioning the identities of people with a learning difficulty and their families – particularly in the organization's early years – Mencap challenged many of the entrenched assumptions upon which British learning disability policy and services had been based. The organization has also battled repeatedly with national and local statutory authorities over cuts to services, as well as effecting change through negotiation and conciliation with different arms of the state sector. It has used its size and status to innovate and provide new learning disability services which have fed directly into statutory provision on a number of occasions over the course of its history. Mencap adopted a discourse of resistance from its earliest years, and this approach has continued to be a vital tool in aiding its growth, and retaining its profile.

However, Mencap itself has also been the object of resistance – both from within and beyond its own organizational structures. Developments in self-advocacy and shifting assumptions about the rights of people with learning difficulties created complex tensions among different stakeholders within the organization, which have frequently been played out at the interface between the national society and its local branches. But these tensions have also led to a reappraisal of some of the inherent suppositions that society has held in the post-war era about the role of voluntary organizations such as Mencap in representing people with learning difficulties.

This chapter, primarily focusing on the period from 1970 onwards, will argue that resistance in its various forms has presented Mencap with numerous challenges as it has been both a target of, and an agent of, resistance. On occasions these challenges have aided Mencap's central objective to improve the lives of people with learning difficulties and their carers. However, resistance has also resulted in many complex internal changes within Mencap itself. As the target of resistance over the past 20 years, the organization has undergone a period of self-reflection about the ways in which its own historical development stimulated a growing body of voices within the learning disability field to question the core values and beliefs of its members.

A note on the sources

This chapter has emerged from an in-depth study of the national Mencap archives, predominantly in the form of publicity material produced by the organization from the 1960s to the 1990s (such as newsletters, magazines, advertisements and annual reports). My analysis of resistance in Mencap's history has also been informed by local Mencap society publications, as well as the data I collected in oral history interviews with several local groups between 2000 and 2001. I have also drawn upon previous academic research undertaken on Mencap's history, particularly work which explores the origins of the national association (Walmsley 2000) and the research into the historical experience of Mencap's local societies (Rolph 2002).

The early years – resisting the status quo

From its beginnings in 1946, the National Association for the Parents of Backward Children (NAPBC), as Mencap was formerly known, was a campaigning organization (Walmsley 2000, p.107). The primary aim of the association from its beginnings was to secure an education for children with learning difficulties, at a time when provision was limited (Shennan 1980, p.10). The organization also pressed for regular and practical help for mothers caring for their children at home. Members resisted the assumption that their children could not be educated and that families should be left with no support from the state. As Judy Fryd, the founding parent of the NAPBC, commented in 1975: 'When we first started, for the majority of our children throughout the country it was a choice between admission to an institution or a mental deficiency hospital, and staying at home in the sole care of his mother' (Fryd 1975, p.13). The 'excluding welfare state' has also been cited as a factor that spurred parents into action in the late 1940s. It soon became apparent to parents of children with learning difficulties in a number of counties that their children were not eligible for many of the benefits of Britain's newly founded NHS (National Health Service) system and they were often still unable to access education services even within special schools (Rolph 2002, 2005).

In 1952, *Parents Voice* (the organization's official magazine) reported that the organization had decided to hold a referendum at its national conference on the question of transferring the education of all disabled children from the Health to the Education Authorities. Two years later the association's official status was recognized and the society was invited to give evidence to the Royal Commission on Mental Illness and Mental Deficiency. For over two hours in their presentation to the Commission, the organization insisted on mandatory powers for local authorities to provide education and training facilities, and hostel accommodation for those who needed it. Although many of these issues were not satisfactorily addressed in the subsequent Mental Health Act of 1959, the archives suggest that Mencap's strategy of resisting the status quo in learning disability services was slowly beginning to infiltrate policy developments in the post-war years, even if it took another decade for the organization's principal aims to come to fruition in official legislation.

Alongside its campaigns around universal education and improved community-care-based services, the National Society for Mentally Handicapped Children (NSMHC), as it became in 1955, was also setting up innovative residential and training projects across the country, with the aim of demonstrating the efficacy of such working examples to local service providers. Throughout the 1950s and 1960s the organization funded a respite home at Orchard Dene in Lancashire, the Brooklands Experiment at the Fountain Hospital under Jack Tizard and the NSMHC National Hostel and Training Centre in Slough. Such experiments established the NSMHC internationally as a progressive and pioneering voluntary organization within the field. They were not designed to supplement inadequate statutory provision, but rather to provide the authorities with models for future improved services.

The new challenges of the 1970s

In 1971, the Chairman of the NSMHC, Lord Segal, commented:

> Today we are still painfully aware of how much more yet remains to be done. We can, however, face the future with some degree of confidence. Let us now redouble our efforts to achieve even greater progress in the years to come. (*Parents Voice* 1971, p.5)

But what form would these 'efforts' take? The period around 1970 was something of a watershed for the organization and the publication of their 1969 annual report, entitled *Turning Point*, indicates an awareness within the NSMHC that their organizational remit was changing (NSMHC 1969). This was prompted by the government's decision to transfer the responsibility for the education and training of people with learning difficulties from the Department of Health and Social Services to the Department of Education and Science in the 1970 Education Act. The organization had campaigned extensively for this legislation, fighting to persuade the authorities that learning disability was not a medical problem to be dealt with under the aegis of doctors, but rather a social phenomenon that necessitated a broad-based education programme and occupational training (Shennan 1980). The passing of this Act subsequently brought about a shift in the national organization's objectives.

New priorities emerged following public reports of neglect and abuse in some of Britain's learning disability hospitals. The NSMHC found itself on the eve of the 1970s responding to the urgent issue of residential care services, acting as the principal voice of a non-statutory body concerned with learning disability.

Following these reports and the publication of Pauline Morris's (1969) *Put Away*, a sociological study financed by the NSMHC, Colonel Verburgh, the organization's vice-chairman, stressed that if the society did not keep up the pressure on the authorities to ensure improved hospital conditions and the rapid provision of hostels within the community 'all the enthusiasm which is at present being displayed by the Government and the hospitals in question will become just so much hot air, particularly if, after the next general election, a new Government takes office' (Verburgh 1970, p.27). The growing links between the NSMHC and other international groups involved in the field, particularly the Danish National Mental Retardation Service – a body promoting legislation which aimed at normalization and integration – undoubtedly reinforced the society's enthusiasm to target the authorities for better residential provisions.

The publicity material produced at this time emphasized that the NSMHC did not see its role as a direct service provider but rather as a parent-oriented consumer body (Parents Voice 1970, p.9). It had long been acknowledged by the national organization that local branches of the society were involved in running services within their community that ranged from the provision of welfare visitors to social clubs for leisure activities (Rolph 2002). Some were going further and investing significant funds in the development of residential homes and training centres for their communities; these were managed either by local branch members or alternatively by local authority employees (Rolph 2005). These local societies were going beyond the language of resistance and were pooling resources for bricks-and-mortar-based projects. A Cambridge society member reported on the progress of the Cambridge hostel that had been open some time, and argued that 'if we get 20–25 years of hostel care from our project, it will be hostel care which we would not otherwise have had' (Parents Voice 1970, p.9). The NSMHC accepted such developments as part of the role of local societies in dealing with their own parochial needs. An official line was negotiated in which the national organization agreed to champion the provision of hostels and other projects by local societies, provided the cooperation of the local authorities was assured. The NSMHC continued to emphasize the importance of its own role for political and lobby-based resistance.

Economic crisis

The NSMHC had begun the 1970s by launching the national society's 'Subnormality in the Seventies' programme that underlined the organization's campaigning priority, stating that 'the task [residential provision] is too large for the long-term answer to be provided in piecemeal fashion by any voluntary system, however powerful' (Solly 1971, p.7). However, as the decade wore on, the organization found itself expending increasing amounts of time and energy resisting threats to services as a direct result of Britain's deepening economic crisis. The situation came to a head in the early 1980s with the stark realization that people with learning difficulties and their families would not survive the government's proposed cuts in public services, notably targeted at social services departments. These cuts provoked a sharp debate about Britain's mixed economy of care that continues to preoccupy academics and politicians today (Hadley and Hatch 1981; HMSO 1988; HMT 2002; Lewis 1993; Means and Smith 1998). The nuances of such arguments were not lost on those working in the voluntary sector. Throughout the 1980s, the National Society for Mentally Handicapped Children and Adults (as it was renamed in 1980, and it will be referred to hereafter as 'Mencap') was forced to reflect upon its position as a lobby group in British politics and consider whether or not this would be compromised by expanding its role as a care provider in the shifting economic and political climate.

After much contention at different levels of the organization, national Mencap chose to meet the task of providing services itself, under the massive Homes Foundation project in which the organization built and managed a significant number of residential centres across the country in conjunction with local authorities. Cries from some quarters in the organization that national Mencap was 'working with the enemy' suggested that a number of members held concerns that Mencap was moving away from its powerful position as 'resistor', towards a place in which its independence as a voluntary body would be compromised. National Mencap countered these fears with various articles in *Parents Voice* which championed the notion of 'Parents as Partners' (Rix 1980/81; Saxon 1982; Whynn Jones 1980), and provided examples in which local society members were successfully 'filling in the gaps' of services for people with learning difficulties. A discourse which aimed to professionalize the carers of people with learning difficulties was used to claw back what was seen by many as lost ground in the fight for improved services. The society was aware that some members might regret the passing of the early pioneering days, but emphasized that the organization now had an obligation to help where it could. But there was a sense amongst some members that entering into this 'partnership' with the state sector would somehow compromise the organization's identity – one which was heavily determined by its distinctly campaign-orientated, resistance-based approach.

The founding of the Homes Foundation scheme signifies the beginning of a period in which tensions between the national body and its local branches proliferated in a more overt way. Despite claims from the centre that these residential projects had brought Mencap into closer contact with the political system, oral history interviews conducted by the author in 2000 suggest that many members shared the belief that this shift actually depoliticized the organization. The distancing that occurred between the centre and local groups over this debate widened over the course of the 1980s and early 1990s and became bound up in a web of new issues.

The search for brand loyalty

The repositioning of Mencap as a prominent service provider in the 1980s brought the question of funding into sharp relief. An editorial in *Parents Voice* from 1986 asserted:

> Fundraising amongst charities is becoming increasingly competitive. The general public are being exposed more and more to appeals from a wider range of causes than ever before… The overall concept of mental handicap is uncomfortable for many people because they feel confused, afraid and ignorant about the subject… Consequently, Mencap is a charity issue of lower priority in people's reasoning. (Parents Voice 1986, p.3)

From its conception, Mencap was highly aware of the issues surrounding the presentation of its constituents as well as its own organizational image. In the early years, the organization found itself dealing with the public's general lack of awareness on the issues surrounding learning disability, as well as people's fear of such individuals, often borne out of the assumption that 'subnormality' was akin to mental illness. An overspill from the eugenics debate had also led to an implicit understanding amongst the public that 'subnormality' was a hereditary condition associated with crime, immorality and disease (Jones 1982; Thomson 1998). From the outset, the organization drew a direct link between the need to change these perceptions in order to secure better services. Ideas about community care were to be made acceptable through promoting an image of people with learning difficulties as pitiful individuals in need of help and support, most memorably in the charity logo 'Little Stephen', which served the national organization from 1957 to 1992 and is still used today in some local societies. The organization turned to public sympathies in order to raise funds for services, portraying people with learning difficulties as helpless beings, deserving compassion and understanding, but also as 'eternal children, inordinately dependent on charity and pity' (Evans 1992, p.139).

By the 1980s, this powerful discourse of the harmless, dependent community of the 'mentally handicapped' was tied more closely than ever with Mencap's fundraising wing and the organization's growing consciousness of its 'corporate' profile. Advertising was afforded increasing emphasis as a means of securing funds for the Homes Foundation project. The nature of these advertising campaigns has been discussed and criticized in some depth over the past few years, the accusation being that the advertisements' disempowering depiction of people with learning difficulties inadvertently damaged the very group that they were supposed to represent (Doddington, Jones and Miller 1994). However, such dilemmas were evident to Mencap at the time, and the organization's predicament was illustrated by its secretary-general, Brian Rix, in 1984:

> On the one hand we must present a positive image of mentally handicapped people, to persuade the public to accept them as friends and neighbours. On the other, we must encourage the view that extra resources in the form of state funds and voluntary donations should be made to meet their special needs. (Rix 1984, p.5)

Mencap attempted to resolve this paradox with the deployment of a number of stark images of disability which were intended to manipulate the viewer into an emotional response of pity. However, this endeavour to 'present positive images of mentally handicapped people' was heavily criticized for portraying the individuals on the posters in either a pathetic or disturbing way. The poster entitled 'No sense, no feelings? They may not think as fast but they feel as deeply' came under particular attack for its insensitive depiction of a couple with learning difficulties. Jessica Evans argues that this advertisement 'presents us with the attitude of the prejudiced viewer which the photograph and the text are supposed to refute' (Evans 1992, p.138). She goes on to give a detailed analysis of the photograph, describing how everything about it exudes negative impressions about intellectual impairment:

> They [the couple] are photographed with a wide angled lens which, when used in close-up, project lips, noses and hands into the viewer's space... The use of top lighting casts shadows into their eyes... The effect is semi-Gothic... The poster indicates that this is the 'handicapped character', who is slightly mad, certainly very peculiar, and who tries to pass as normal by aspiring to the honorific portrait and institution of marriage. (Evans 1992, p.138)

One consequence of these campaigns was the decision by some members of the organization to leave Mencap and join other existing organizations or alternatively set up their own groups – a significant example of resistance from within. But such actions went beyond the criticism of one particular advertising campaign. Resistance to the images and language adopted by Mencap in its representation of people with learning difficulties was so pertinent because it was striking at the very core of the organization's values and beliefs about learning disability. The advertising campaigns were seen as an outward manifestation of the underlying assumptions within Mencap that people with learning difficulties were not capable or desiring of independence, even within a supported framework. The images and the discourse constituted by Mencap in the 1980s were coming to be seen as symbols of a past historical era, and were resisted by younger voluntary organizations eager to reposition attitudes towards learning disability once again.

Self-advocacy

Some of the younger voluntary groups mentioned above were other parent-based organizations, but a growing voice could also be heard from a number of advocacy and self-advocacy groups (Williams and Shoultz 1982). The prominence of the service user provided such groups with a powerful platform from which to approach the issue of representation within learning disability organizations. This went beyond the issue of *how* people were being represented and explored – perhaps more fundamentally – the question of *who* was being represented. Were the main stakeholders in Mencap, for example, actually the *carers* of people with learning difficulties? It seemed to those both outside the organization and those within it that parents were speaking *on behalf* of their children, because if they didn't, then who would? However, the growth of self-advocacy in a variety of settings was contributing to a notion already gaining currency in scholarly debate that people with learning difficulties could not only *speak for themselves*, but also had the right to participate in decisions that would impact upon their lives (Atkinson and Williams 1990; Crawley 1988; Shearer 1986).

Interestingly (and this is sometimes forgotten), Mencap did provide both the funding and the administrative base for one of the earliest self-advocacy groups in the UK. The participation forum, set up in 1981 by the London divisional office, brought together a network of people working through self-advocacy groups and committees in day centres and other settings, although it was not a formally constituted self-advocacy body and lacked an organized representative structure (Shearer 1986, p.187). The participation forum tackled a range of personal and social issues around learning disability in the 1980s and also acted in an advisory role to other fledgling self-advocacy groups. However, its expansion was limited by the moderate funds it received, which in 1986 still did not permit the employment of a full-time adviser.

Despite the founding of this informal group, Mencap did not forcefully address the issue of self-advocacy until the 1990s, when it was becoming increasingly clear that Mencap was perceived as conservative and resistant to change by other learning disability organizations such as People First and RADAR (The Royal Association for Disablement and Rehabilitation). In 1983 a group of self-advocates from Essex campaigned against Mencap's use of the Little Stephen logo arguing that 'the little boy makes people think we are lost, lonely, sad, miserable and pathetic... We can't change people's minds about us if you carry on showing us up to the public' (Shearer 1986, p.181). In the early 1990s, members of People First groups were writing to Mencap's magazine, complaining about the organization's use of terminology such as 'mental handicap' and 'learning disabilities', and proposing instead the adoption of 'learning difficulties' in future publicity material (Bull 1992). Other People First groups were campaigning to have the Little Stephen logo removed from mini-buses (Johnstone 1991). Additionally, the growth of specific organizations in the 1980s for people with learning difficulties, such as the Down Syndrome Association, meant that Mencap was losing significant support from a number of parents and carers. This, alongside the growing criticism from rights-based organizations, forced Mencap to question the fundamental basis on which its future depended. Mencap had to consider whether it could continue to exist as an organization *for* people with learning difficulties, or whether it would have to remould itself into an organization *of* people with learning difficulties.

Changing representations: A question of who and how?

In 1992 Mencap underwent a relaunch with the aim to revolutionize and update the society's image. The 'Little Stephen' logo was dropped and replaced with five photographic images of real people. The new logos aimed to be inclusive, representing the wide range of Mencap's beneficiaries in terms of age, gender and race, and showed people experiencing life either singly or in a couple. The society also rethought their use of terminology, which had become an intrinsic component of its staid image. After much debate, it was agreed that Mencap would drop the use of descriptions such as 'mental handicap' and replace them with terminology such as 'learning disability' or 'difficulty', which was much more acceptable to people with learning difficulties themselves. An article published in the Mencap magazine attempted to explain to members why the national committee had decided to initiate such a major image conversion. It explained that Mencap had to be seen to be moving with the times, and it fully accepted past criticisms concerning its representations of people with learning difficulties (Parents Voice 1992, p.8).

The extent to which the relaunch was accepted throughout the local societies varied enormously. In a number of small rural societies around the country the previous terminology is still in use today, and Little Stephen can be found on groups' publicity material. The interviews that I undertook with local society members in 2000–2001 demonstrated a range of views on the subject of this relaunch, with many having decided to implement the new policies after 'getting used to the changes' during the 1990s. Some groups argued that national Mencap should have initiated the changes before 1992 – indeed they had been anticipating the new direction for a number of years. Most interviewees, both at a national and local level, agreed that Mencap did have a responsibility towards its older members, many of whom found it very difficult to consent to the changes. Participants observed that this cohort of elderly parents had worked tremendously hard in the past to bring about provisions when no support existed. It also became clear through the course of these interviews that many of the anxieties held by some older members resonated throughout the organization. Concerns about the place of people with multiple and profound learning difficulties in the new user-orientated climate, and the impact of more community-based services which have left some users and carers without adequate support, were and remain pertinent issues for both new and older parents. The relaunch of 1992 – an event bound up in the developments of the 1980s – brought such questions to the forefront of Mencap's agenda and highlighted tensions about representation and identity that existed amongst the organization's stakeholders.

Constitutional change

The relaunch also forced Mencap to consider other aspects of the organization that had been called into question throughout the 1980s. In 1998, *The Case for Change* was published, explaining the proposed constitutional change that would introduce individual membership, giving members a vote at the annual conference, at constituency level and on district committees (Mencap 1998a). The concept of a National Assembly was put forward with a proposal that over a third of members elected from each region would be people with a learning difficulty. Tim Gadd, Chair of the Membership and Committee Structure Working Party, commented:

> We [Mencap] must continue to grow and develop if we are to meet the needs of more people with a learning disability and their families. An essential part of that development is to ensure that we become a more representative and responsive organisation: involving more people in Mencap and giving people a stake in what we do. (Mencap 1998b)

The visual and linguistic overhaul that Mencap undertook in the 1990s needed to be accompanied by structural changes within the organization if it was to remain a major player in the learning disability field. Formalized links between service users and the central hub of Mencap enshrined the values of inclusion and rights for people with learning difficulties within a high-profile organization and were a powerful indicator that such principles could permeate beyond the remit of self-advocacy groups and the academic literature. The 1992 relaunch, alongside this constitutional restructuring, is also evidence of a large voluntary sector organization at the end of the twentieth century adopting a range of strategic devices from the corporate world in order to operate and survive in an environment that resembles a vastly different landscape today from that of its historical roots.

Conclusion

Mencap's strategy of resistance has stimulated its growth from a small campaigning group to one of Britain's most prominent learning dlisability charities. This resistant approach has encompassed a range of tactics over the past 60 years, many of which have assisted the organization's aim of securing better services for people with learning difficulties. But Mencap has also faced resistance from within its own organizational structures, as well as from service users, parents and academics. The national body has consciously renegotiated its identity as an organization both for and of people with learning difficulties in line with the developments in self-advocacy and user-orientated approaches to services. However, the extent to which this repositioning has infiltrated local societies has varied over the past decade, and the question of who is represented by Mencap in practice (beyond the rhetoric) remains a relevant one. Resistance has been a valuable and recurring tool in Mencap's history – on the one hand allowing it to help change society's attitudes towards learning difficulty, while on the other forcing it to keep up with the very developments that the organization itself had initiated so many years before.

References

Atkinson, D. and Williams, F. (eds) (1990) *Know Me As I Am: An Anthology of Prose, Poetry and Art by People with Learning Difficulties*. London: Hodder and Stoughton.

Bull, N. (1992) 'Letters.' *Mencap News*, May, 2–3.

Crawley, B. (1988) *A Survey of Self-Advocacy Groups in Adult Training Centres and Hospitals in Great Britain*. London: CHM.

Doddington, K., Jones, R.S.P. and Miller, B.Y. (1994) 'Are attitudes to people with learning disabilities negatively influenced by charity advertising? An experimental analysis.' *Disability and Society*, 9 (2), 207–22.

Evans, J. (1992) 'Little Stephen', in D. Hevey (ed.) *The Creatures that Time Forgot – Photography and Disability Imagery*. London: Routledge.

Fryd, J. (1975) 'Twenty-five years on.' *Parents Voice*, September, 13–15.

Hadley, R. and Hatch, S. (1981) *Social Welfare and the Failure of the State*. London: George Allen and Unwin.

HMSO (1988) *Community Care: An Agenda for Action (The Griffiths Report)*. London: HMSO.

HMT (2002) *The Role of the Voluntary and Community Sector in Service Delivery: A Cross Cutting Review*. London: HMT.

Johnstone, V. (1991) 'People First – to speak for themselves.' *Mencap News*, July, 4–5.

Jones, G. (1982) 'Eugenics and social policy between the wars.' *Historical Journal*, 25 (3), 717–28.

Lewis, J. (1993) 'Developing the mixed economy of care: Emerging issues for voluntary organisations.' *Journal of Social Policy*, 22 (2), 173–92.

Means, R. and Smith, R. (1998) *Community Care: Policy and Practice, Second Edition*. Basingstoke: Macmillan.

Mencap (1998a) *The Case for Change*. London: Mencap.

Mencap (1998b) *Securing Our Future*. London: Mencap.

Morris, P. (1969) *Put Away: A Sociological Study of Institutions for the Mentally Retarded*. New York: Atherton Press.

NSMHC (1969) *Turning Point – Annual Report of the NSMHC*. London: NSMHC.

Parents Voice (1952) Editorial. *Parents Voice*, Issue 3.

Parents Voice (1970) 'Members meeting.' *Parents Voice*, December, 9–10.

Parents Voice (1971) 'Twenty-five years: 1946–1971. *Parents Voice*, Autumn, 4–5.

Parents Voice (1986) Editorial. *Parents Voice*, Autumn, 3.

Parents Voice (1992) 'Making the future.' *Mencap News*, November, 8–9.

Rix, B. (1980/81) 'Inaugural address.' *Parents Voice*, winter, 5–6.

Rix, B. (1984) 'How to influence public attitudes.' *Parents Voice*, Autumn, 4–6.

Rolph, S. (2002) *Reclaiming the Past: The Role of Local Mencap Societies in the Development of Community Care in East Anglia, 1946–1980*. Milton Keynes: The Open University.

Rolph, S. (2005) *Captured on Film: The History of Norwich and District Mencap Society, 1954–1990*. Milton Keynes: The Open University.

Saxon, G. (1982) 'Partnership in care.' *Parents Voice*, December, 11–21.

Shearer, A. (1986) *Building Community with People with Mental Handicaps, their Families and Friends*. London: King's Fund and CMH.

Shennan, V. (1980) *Our Concern: The Story of the National Association for Mentally Handicapped Children and Adults*. London: The National Association for Mentally Handicapped Children and Adults.

Solly, K. (1971) 'Subnormality in the seventies: Programme for pressure.' *Parents Voice*, March, 6–7.

Thomson, M. (1998) *The Problem of Mental Deficiency in England and Wales, 1913–1946*. Oxford: Clarendon Press.

Verburgh, G.H. (1970) 'Programme for pressure.' *Parents Voice*, March, 27.

Walmsley, J. (2000) 'Straddling boundaries: The changing roles of voluntary organisations, 1913–1959', in L. Brigham, D. Atkinson, M. Jackson, S. Rolph and J. Walmsley (eds) *Crossing Boundaries: Change and Continuity in the History of Learning Disability*. Worcestershire: BILD.

Williams, P. and Shoultz, B. (1982) *We Can Speak for Ourselves: Self-Advocacy by Mentally Handicapped People*. London: Souvenir Press.

Wynn Jones, A. (1980) 'The turn of the decade.' *Parents Voice*, March, no page numbers.

14

One Man's Dream
that Continues to Inspire Others

Heather Cadbury

Wolfgang Stange is a dance teacher who worked for one day a week for 14 years at Normansfield Hospital near London. Wolfgang worked in the beautiful theatre at Normansfield. The theatre is ornate and richly decorated and was originally built for shows. Wolfgang worked with lots of different people with different abilities. He also organized shows in the theatre in which many people with learning disabilities took part. Wolfgang fought against the bad views of some of the staff and tried to encourage everyone to be involved in dance and theatre.

Introduction

Wolfgang Stange, a choreographer and dance teacher, worked one day a week for 14 years between the mid-1970s and the late 1980s at Normansfield Hospital which is in the outskirts of London. During that time he persisted with learning to communicate with many of the hospital's disabled residents, who were receiving very little stimulation. Their care was mostly custodial and they tended to be viewed as medical curiosities. Wolfgang was employed to inject some creative ideas into this closed community, and for the staff to use some of his ideas.

However, influencing attitudes and the established patterns of work was almost impossible. Research into institutions for learning disabilities reveals staff tend to use a system of rewards and punishment, and in one study carried out in Finland 90 per cent of reinforcement behaviour focused on punishment (Krause and Viemero 1997). This was not a system that Wolfgang could identify with; he concentrated on working with the residents. Trained as a dancer, Wolfgang had no experience of working with disabled people and might easily have walked away from the uphill struggle. Help came from a steady flow of volunteers assisting him on his journey of discovery. Carol Rentoul, a dance teacher, was also involved for many years. Their approach was to develop the students by introducing them to a variety of music and props. This was an interactive method of facilitating movement often initiated by sharing the students' world, learning to see what they saw and to feel what they felt. They then set about extending each individual's world.

Normansfield had an important attraction for a dancer – the beautiful Victorian theatre in which Wolfgang took his classes: 'I was thrilled to have this glorious theatre to work with, I thought…wow! We may as well use it' (Stange 1994). Thus the work of John Langdon-Down, the founder of Normansfield, was over the years to inspire Wolfgang. They shared the same love of and fascination for the theatre. This chapter discusses the founding ideas of Langdon-Down that, although now understood to be at the least paternalistic, nevertheless challenged prevailing ideas about working with people with learning disabilities. It then links them with the work of Wolfgang Stange who, inspired by some of the original ideals of Normansfield, resisted much of what it had become.

Normansfield Hospital – a brief history

Originally Normansfield had been a small private home which opened its doors to 'the backward and feeble minded' in 1868. It was considered by many to be both innovative and caring in its approach. John Langdon-Down believed there was a need to provide a home for children of the rich and wealthy, since institutions at that time were caring for the poor, permitting only a few private patients. He started with only 19 individuals, who lived in the same house as his family, but the number grew at an astonishing rate. Only 11 years later the original house had been extended, with a north and a south wing and the all-important theatre. More ground had been purchased, providing other houses for the more able and an area for an extensive farm. One hundred and thirty seven people now lived at Normansfield. By 1892 the clock tower wing and the conservatory were built and the number of residents had reached 200. The community continued at this size until the final closure programme was initiated.

After John Langdon-Down's death in 1896 Normansfield remained privately run, by the family, during two world wars. However, changes in British society increasingly made financial survival impossible and in 1951 the family sold their home to the NHS. At this stage some staff and a number of residents moved elsewhere. A grandson of the founder, Norman Langdon-Down, remained as the medical superintendent until his retirement in 1970. A psychiatrist was appointed with several managers to assist in the day-to-day running. Evidence suggests that conditions deteriorated rapidly. In 1976 a COHSE (Confederation of Health Service Employees) strike by care staff culminated in the psychiatrist being suspended. Two years later the Sherrard Report blamed both the psychiatrist and the managers for the custodial and poor quality of care provided. The era following this report saw an increased input of both money and expertise. A £1.3 million complex was built, providing an activity centre and two bungalow complexes – more suitable accommodation for the physically disabled. The new management structure had the task of improving the life within this community, preparing everyone for closure and life in the wider community. Changes being implemented at that time were in many respects a return to the type of care once provided by John and Mary Langdon-Down. The doors finally closed in 1997, when residents moved from a large hospital into small community homes.

John Langdon-Down: The founder

In 1868 the philosophy and methods of John Langdon-Down and his wife Mary were extremely enlightened, and evidence suggests he was among a small circle of individuals attempting to improve care of those who were then known as 'feeble-minded'. Having worked at Earlswood for ten years he decided to open his own institution. The opening ceremony was held in June 1879 once most of the building work had been completed. This event was naturally held in the entertainment hall for a large and distinguished audience, including the Earl of Devon. Part of John Langdon-Down's speech provides us with his vision:

> My Lord, – the ceremony in which you are about to take a prominent part this day is the realization of a dream of mine some thirty-three years ago. In a remote part of the country whose name your lordship so worthily bears, driven by the stress of weather from an al fresco picnic into a cottage on the west, I was brought into contact with a feeble-minded girl, who waited on our party, and for whom the question haunted me, – could anything be done?

...to provide the highest possible culture, the best physical, moral, and intel-lectual training, and to open out fresh realms of happiness for a class who have the strongest claims on our sympathy, and for whom until lately so little has been done. (Private scrapbook owned by Patricia Langdon-Down)

In fact, the realization of his dream was eventually completed on a monumental scale. Qualifying late in life to be a doctor and going on to build this large institu-tion was an amazing feat for someone who had come from quite humble begin-nings (Ward 1998). Newspaper reports from that period record the many grand and creative events that John Langdon-Down and his wife hosted. One such event was the Queen's Golden Jubilee which coincided with their son Reginald's 21st birthday:

There were exhibitions of Punch and Judy, at which old as well as young found much amusement, performing dogs &c., and it was not till evening wore on to dusk, and the children had caught a glimpse of the fairyland into which the charming grounds were transformed with variegated lamps that they retired for the night...the grounds presented a charming appearance, the view of the lawns and paths, lit up with fairy lamps, some tracing the edges of the trim-kept grass, others ensconced amid the leafiness of the trees and shrubs, and yet others lining the creeper-covered trellis arches, being quite enchanting... Dancing was pursued with energy upon the turf to the strains of the well-trained band of the institution and the utmost enjoyment prevailed. A bountiful and elaborate supply of refreshments was continu-ously going in one of the large saloons opening out onto the lawn, and at ten o'clock the company, some 250 in number, sat down under the presidency of Dr Down in the handsome apartment known as the kindersaal. (Private scrapbook owned by Patricia Langdon-Down)

This write-up of events conveys images of wealth, creativity and also indicates the loyalty of some of the staff. There are also many similar and lengthy newspaper articles describing performances held in the tiny Victorian theatre, including the annual Christmas show. The theatrical performances, like the Jubilee celebrations, must have provided a magical setting. The flickering gas light and the expertly hand-painted scenery is thought by many theatrical historians to have provided a unique quality unrivalled by the electric lighting which took its place at a later date.

The entertainment hall

In stark contrast to this luxury, the exterior of the entertainment hall, as it was called, looks quite austere, perhaps reminiscent of a Methodist chapel. Indeed on Sundays the hall was used for church services. Scenery was replaced by a special cloth on which the Lord's Prayer was printed and a lectern was used for conducting the services. Religion undoubtedly played an important part in the lives of John and Mary Langdon-Down, but they were also passionate about acting and the theatre.

During the late nineteenth century a large number of amateur concerts were held in the Borough of Richmond, many of which were used as fundraising events. Local archives reveal newspaper cuttings and programmes of such events, which indicate a large number of musicians, actors, singers and song writers, many of whom became involved with Normansfield and their productions. This was after all prior to the British Broadcasting Corporation, which started up in 1926, so communities provided their own entertainment.

Rowland Plumbe, a friend known from the Earlswood days, was employed as the architect for the theatre. Although he had no experience in designing theatres, he was noted for being the chief architect for the London Hospital, its medical school and a number of housing estates (Earl 1997). The hall itself was built on the first floor, the ground floor being the *kindersaal* or play area for the children. This beautiful Victorian theatre is ornate and richly decorated, particularly the wall which supports the stage or proscenium. The other three walls on the inside are constructed with plain brick leading up to a beautifully carved vaulted ceiling consisting of pine trusses. The original elegant sun-burner or gas light remains in its central position. The balcony at the rear of the theatre is decorated with ornamental ironwork, which also features on the staircases leading to the proscenium, and the front of the forestage is decorated with 15 individually painted panels. However, it is the wall surrounding the stage which is most extravagantly decorated with gold etching and elaborate paintings. Two of the panels, continuous with each staircase, are doors leading to the wings and backstage. Above each door are two paintings of life-sized figures depicting tragedy, painting, music and comedy (Earl 1997).

There remains to this day an extensive collection of stock scenery, scenery that can be adapted for different plays, as opposed to being created for only one production. Although too fragile to use today, originally the scenery would have floated on an amazingly simple system of grooves. 'Scenic flats', as they were called, glided on or off stage, when scene changes were necessary. In later years the stage remained adorned only in simple flowing curtains. Wolfgang never saw

Normansfield Theatre (courtesy of The Theatres Trust; photograph: David Willmot)

the wealth of Victorian scenery hidden away untouched for years. It was the theatre itself which motivated Wolfgang in his work.

Wolfgang Stange
Callisthenics

Initially Wolfgang worked with the less disabled residents at Normansfield. However, once the new activity centre was opened he lost all his students and he started to work with the more severely disabled:

> So one day I came to my class and all my students had gone, nobody was there and nobody informed me the week before even. They had a new occupational therapist, I am sad to say. She never even told me they had to go to different units to do their work. (Stange 1994)

Wolfgang was allowed his students back for the performance and after that he had to start again with a totally different group of students. Carol Rentoul remembers how some would return when they could:

I remember one woman putting on a long cloak, Wolfgang played slow music. The woman walked slowly round the room moving in a dream to the sounds. The music really reached her; it was very touching. (Rentoul 1993, p.28)

His new group included people needing wheelchairs and those who had very little concentration or communication skills. Some students wandered aimlessly round the hall, others sat rocking in a corner. One particular individual made a dash to rip out the toilet if the opportunity arose. Another might be seen frozen halfway down the stairs until someone told him what to do. Each week Wolfgang arrived with new ideas and materials from different countries, determined to use his creative skills to reach his students who may have spent their entire life being told what to do, where to go and when to do it. He actively encouraged them to experience a range of emotions and to express their feelings.

The sessions included a warm-up period where people just greeted one another and socialized. Wolfgang would then proceed through a series of exercises, often using music to facilitate movement, allowing the individuals freedom to develop skills which they initiated. Each session finished with a period of calm relaxation, the students lying on the floor listening to music before they dispersed back to the wards.

The exercises were many and varied. At times students worked in pairs creating static shapes with their bodies, sometimes they incorporated a piece of equipment or just a piece of material. Some performed better if their work gained an anonymous quality and the use of material or a mask could often satisfy that need. On other occasions bodily shapes might be formed round a central focus by the whole group, once again incorporating props or equipment. At times pairs acted out a particular scene such as a fight or a dance which was often accompanied by music.

For those individuals who found physical closeness unbearable, volunteers would mimic their repetitive movements. Some were so amazingly intricate that many volunteers found it impossible to mirror the exact complexity. Other students who just wandered were followed at an acceptable distance, often for weeks until they progressed to a closer and more trusting relationship.

Residents unable to walk were allowed to enjoy expressing themselves to music, using their wheels as feet. Volunteers made the chairs dance, and the individuals were able to feel the sensations of twirling, and tilting in time with the music. Carol noted:

> We danced with residents by holding their arms and allowing them to feel how the music made us dance. Their faces used to slowly relax and one could feel their tensions drifting away. (Rentoul 1993, p.28)

At times residents were taken out of their chairs and would be held by others allowing these students to experience how music can be interpreted by the whole body. Research has indicated just how important touch is for people in institutional care (le May 1999). Personal care in institutions is often performed in a cold impersonal manner. For the students learning to express themselves without the use of language, dance is a particularly useful skill. Carol stated: 'Students gradually learn control over their bodies, and then through dance movements – their own – they slowly learn to express themselves' (Rentoul 1993, p.26).

Wolfgang admits he sometimes found it hard to get people to dance for themselves, until he devised a method for one student who was continually asking for approval: 'I gave him a tape case to hold and told him to look at it, not at me while he danced. Every time he tried to ask I just said look at the case. I had to keep it up for quite a few weeks. I wanted him to find his own focus' (Stange 1994, p.30).

Productions

Soon after his arrival at Normansfield Wolfgang directed and staged original performances in the Victorian theatre. A part of John Langdon-Down's community was once again in use, providing pleasure and entertainment to residents, staff and relatives, only this time, the majority of the performers had learning difficulties. The first year (1975) he used the story of the Nativity:

> But even then I loved them to listen to different sounds of music, and they went on at this early stage to listen to classical music. I remember I used the Christmas Oratorio by Bach for the opening. We had Michael, he had the face of an angel, so therefore I put him as the Archangel Gabriel. He had such a beautiful face. It was easy for him to be just himself, he could go from A to B, if he forgot others helped him so there was no problem. Joseph became Joseph, not because of his name but he was friendly with Gillian and she became Mary. All the parents came and lots of staff. (Stange 1994, p.30)

The following year Wolfgang elaborated on the basic Nativity story by adding a multicultural dimension. His story contained themes of tolerance and used examples of what each country has to offer in the way of music and customs, which were discovered by the characters during their long journey following the star:

> we went on to do the *Friendship Journey*. I devised it because in the meantime I introduced a little Japanese music and Indian music. Even if I played different music they could identify it was from Japan. People saw a star in different countries of Europe and they wanted to find out the message of the star, so they went first by train and we used the Train Polka by Strauss and they all had different flags. All the countries came together from Europe and took the train to India. Then we had Indian dancers with the hands, then they asked them to join them and they took a boat from India to Japan, yet other customs and music...and so the Japanese joined also, but the Japanese being more advanced went by plane. The plane crashed and landed in the jungle. Sally was the medicine man. The fear they had of this strange creature subsided and they became friends and they all went to the star. I brought in two friends who were dancers and actors and they spoke the words of the Lord Buddha and Jesus. They all did a friendship dance together. (Stange 1994, p.31)

Wolfgang was asked if he and his actors could provide a repeat performance in 1977 as part of the celebrations for the Queen's Silver Jubilee. Shortly before the performance Wolfgang was asked to attend the Inquiry into Normansfield Hospital to discuss his relationship with the psychiatrist, who had been suspended. As usual Wolfgang was determined to make the best of the situation and invited the Board of Inquiry to his play. On this occasion the actors had some important and distinguished people in the audience, since the members of the board all turned up.

Over the years Wolfgang discovered many people who were eager to assist both with his classes and his productions, whilst others continued to make life difficult for him. Rumours and fears that the actors would be drugged or merely not allowed to turn up for performances were rife; luckily this never happened. His final production, first performed in 1980, was described in the programme as 'A reflection in dance, poetry and drama of the handicaps, mental, physical, visual, emotional, which beset us all' and was titled *I Am Not Yet Dead*. The idea of using disability as the focus had evolved from the integration work with a dance group that he now ran in the community. His students had all sorts of disabilities including blindness, a particularly challenging student for a choreographer. Wolfgang had some rehearsals at Normansfield and the kitchen obligingly provided tea and biscuits for everybody. The performance was a great success and the theatre was packed with an appreciative audience of relatives and local people. The sting came later when Wolfgang was billed £78.50 for the tea and biscuits. Eventually after a long struggle he was allowed not to pay, but only when he threatened to charge for all the overtime he had put in – and at his London rate, not the minimal rate paid by the health authority.

Undoubtedly the hardest battle, and the most tiring on a day-to-day basis, was with the negative attitudes of staff. However, Wolfgang recalled how a particular incident made him more determined:

> I intended to take the Normansfield people to the Commonwealth Institute, there was a big Sri Lanka exhibition on and since you know my love for Sri Lanka, I wanted to share some of that. They knew the music by then, I had brought the masks in, I brought in other artefacts... So at this point Carol brought a small globe in. One of the male nurses stood in the corner and watched all this. David of course could say globe and Graham could say G...L...O...B...E and I said 'Up here is England and down there is Sri Lanka'. As I said that the male nurse said, 'What the f... hell do they know, what a f... globe is?' and walked out.
>
> Of course when people do come in like that you feel slightly nervous and you wonder if you are going over the top, maybe it is true there is no point in explaining this. So I decided we should all become the world and make a round shape. So we went to the Commonwealth Institute about three weeks later and we went to see the exhibition. There was a lecture on in the afternoon with colour slides and some Kandyan dancing with costumes. We had hardly sat down and one of the students started rocking, and I felt terrible and so Carol looked at me and I looked at Carol, and the woman next to him started moving on. The rocking backwards and forwards got fiercer, now I really got quite worried because I thought something was irritating him and I said to Carol I would take him out. I hardly said it and he jumped up and ran across the floor and the lecturer leaped to the side and he ran over to the table and I just about caught him there, he stood there and pointed and said 'G...L...O...B...E!' On the table was an enormous globe. (Stange 1994, p.39–40)

Conclusion

In this chapter Wolfgang Stange represents many people who have resisted prevailing views about people with learning disabilities. In his case, he had to contend with systems that devalued people and with workers who had become contemptuous about the abilities of people they worked with. Many such workers were ground down by the atmosphere of Normansfield that, despite having been founded on idealism, had become, like so many institutions, oppressive places in which to live. Stange stood out from many others in that he was inspired by the original idealism and therefore resisted the prevailing atmosphere.

References

Earl, J. (1997) *Dr Langdon-Down and the Normansfield Theatre.* Twickenham: Borough of Twickenham Local History Society.

Krause, C. and Viemero, V. (1997) 'What really happened in the institutional care of mentally retarded people 1982–1991.' *Psykologia,* 32 (6), 435–44.

le May, A. (1999) *Touch in Older Age.* Nursing Times Clinical Monographs. London: EMAP.

Rentoul, C. (1993) Normansfield Project – an unpublished oral history project. Teddington Area Reminiscence Group, Teddington Library, Middlesex.

Stange, W. (1994) Normansfield Project – an unpublished oral history project. Teddington Area Reminiscence Group, Teddington Library, Middlesex.

Ward, C. (1998) *John Langdon Down: A Caring Pioneer.* Dorchester: Dorset Press.

15

Maureen Oswin and the 'Forgotten Children' of the Long-stay Wards

Research as Resistance

Sheena Rolph and Dorothy Atkinson

Maureen Oswin helped to make sure that children were no longer put into long-stay hospitals. She did this through her research. This meant that she spent a lot of time looking at what happened in the children's wards of long-stay hospitals. She discovered that children had very little privacy and very little time from the nurses. She made a lot of notes so that she could prove that what she said was right. Many people were angry at Maureen for writing about the bad conditions for children in hospital and they tried to say that she was not right. Maureen had to fight hard to be heard but her work helped to change things for people with learning difficulties.

Introduction

The late Maureen Oswin spent several years of her working life in the back wards of the long-stay mental disability hospitals. Initially a teacher of children with high-support needs, she later became a researcher in residential and institutional settings where, largely forgotten, children lived out their childhoods and often their whole lives. These were the 'Cinderellas of a Cinderella service', a subgroup of institutionalized children who were living the most isolated and deprived lives imaginable. Maureen's research involved her in systematic and meticulous observation of the day-to-day lives of children in the so-called special care wards of the long-stay hospitals.

Research into the lives of deprived children on the back wards might have disappeared into obscurity. This is, after all, the fate of much research. This research was different, however. It was published in the 1970s amidst much accompanying publicity and it created a storm. Unusually again, it was research that made a difference. Not many years later, the admission of children to long-stay hospitals ceased completely.

What led Maureen Oswin into giving up first her weekends, then later her working life, to researching and publicizing the plight of these children? We briefly explore the historical context in which Maureen's research emerged and we attempt to retrace her personal journey into it. A key issue in this is Maureen the person and how she became the champion and advocate of the children she set out to study. It is important to note in this context that Maureen did not embark on a study of 'resistance'. This is, however, the linking theme of this book and we have used it to revisit Maureen's original field notes (now held in the Open University Archives: OUA) and her subsequent publications. We found in our archival search and book rereading that resistance featured in Maureen's research at several levels.

At one level, there are Maureen's observations of daily life, the research notes she kept every day. All too often she was recording the deprivation of children but also where appropriate (and sadly, rarely) she was recording the *small acts of resistance* in others. At another level, Maureen reflected on her findings even as she wrote them, criticizing and refusing to accept the poor conditions and bad practices that she witnessed and recorded. In some instances, Maureen not only criticized what she saw, she tried to change it by timely *interventions* on behalf of the children and their families.

In her role of researcher, Maureen recorded the apparent *lack of resistance* on the part of the people charged with caring for the children. At the same time, though, she sought to explain this phenomenon by identifying the *barriers to resistance*. She noted the factors that stopped people caring – or even noticing – what deprived lives the children were leading. When her findings were published, Maureen's voice as a *critical researcher* was heard alongside her detailed observations of children's lives in the long-stay hospitals. Finally, in later years, Maureen reflected on the *cost of resistance* to herself. She was a 'whistle-blower' before there was such a term or concept and she paid dearly for it. So why did she do it? Why did she resist what she witnessed when others did not? We suggest some possible reasons. We explore each of these topics, drawing on unpublished archived field notes from Maureen's original research as well as from her subsequent published work.

Setting the context for resistance

Maureen arrived at Queen Mary's Hospital in Carshalton, Surrey, in 1959. The timing was propitious, as 1959 saw the passing of the Mental Health Act, which repealed the old Mental Deficiency Act of 1913 and held out hope of a new and more humane approach to people with learning difficulties. The new Act was the result of a decade of debate about 'mental deficiency', and growing concerns as to government policy regarding the huge institutions and the many thousands of people living – certified and detained – within them. (According to Korman and Glennerster (1990), in 1939 there were 46,054 people – including children – living in institutions, and by the mid-1960s there were 64,000.) The concerns had been triggered at the start of the decade in 1951 by the National Council for Civil Liberties (NCCL) whose pamphlet, *50,000 Outside the Law,* pointed to the inhumane treatment of people in hospitals and the human rights abuses carried out in the name of the 1913 Act.

In 1954, a Royal Commission was appointed to investigate these concerns. The 1959 Act was the outcome of the debates instigated by the Commission. It signalled changed attitudes: it abolished the classifications of 'idiot', 'imbecile', 'feeble-minded' and 'moral defective', replacing them with 'subnormal' and 'severely subnormal'; and it encouraged a move away from institutions to community care. There was still no acknowledgement, however, that children should have the right to education: many were still excluded as 'ineducable', even if they were lucky enough to have special schools in their area, and stayed at home, went to one of the few occupation centres or were admitted to an institution.

It was with the knowledge of the new Act, as well as the NCCL pamphlet, that Maureen took up her post as teacher at Queen Mary's. Although primarily a hospital for sick children it gradually began to accept many children with severe physical as well as learning disabilities. She very soon discovered that the beautiful setting of 'acres of lovely grounds...with trees, lawns and flowerbeds...with separate red-brick villas' belied what was taking place on the children's wards:

> There was no privacy, not even in the lavatories... Their life style was very abnormal. They never went out of the hospital... The children were lucky if they had a cuddle or if they had any staff who stayed long enough to really get to know them. They lived totally institutionalised lives, excluded from the rest of society. (Oswin 2000, pp.136–37)

Maureen's reaction was to resist the regime and defy the workings of the law:

> Gradually I began to get the occasional child with severe learning disabilities in my little group of children with cerebral palsy. The current Education Act [1944] did not include 'severely abnormal children' in ordinary education, so by accepting children with severe learning disabilities into my group I was stretching the Education laws... Gradually I began to criticise the care of the children in my particular ward. (Oswin 2000, p.138)

Her criticism provoked defensive – even horrified – reactions from her fellow teachers, and she became increasingly unpopular for challenging the system. It seemed that no-one else was willing to entertain the thought that the treatment of the children was damaging. The head teacher told Maureen 'But *these* sort of children do not GO OUT', and the other teachers warned her not to get 'emotionally involved with the children'. She continued to challenge the regime, however, writing not only to the hospital management committee but also to Enoch Powell, Minister of Health, asking for better accommodation for the school room. There were two results. The first was that the head teacher told her she was 'mad' and would be black-listed, barred from promotion. The second was that she was gradually successful in obtaining small concessions for the children, such as 'regular outings to town, bits of furniture for the bedroom, and even a tiny cooker in my school-room so they could enjoy mixing up flour to make cakes' (Oswin 2000, p.139).

At St Mary's it appears that the staff were still operating according to philosophies enshrined in the 1913 Act. The teachers, too, followed the 1944 Education Act to the letter, denying more ambitious educational opportunities to many children, and refusing to allow them to visit the outside world. During her time at St Mary's, Maureen challenged the regime in several ways. She ignored the rules; she complained to her immediate boss, the head teacher; she also wrote to the highest hospital officials; and, finally, she made representations outside the hospital to the highest authority of all, the Minister of Health. This was done at a personal cost. However, the small concessions she won for the children were encouraging and paved the way for further patterns of resistance on-site by

Maureen in the many other hospitals she visited in the course of her research, a point we return to below.

Developing a pattern of resistance: Keeping detailed research notes

Maureen's weekends of part-time research, and later her longer research projects with Jack Tizard at the Thomas Coram Research Unit, took her over the next 20 years to many other hospitals, homes or boarding schools. During all these visits and stays, she made long and detailed notes of everything she observed on the wards or in the hospital schools, adding headings and indexes. This in itself was an act of resistance, as she realized the value of all this material and the use to which it could be put in the battle to improve conditions and change attitudes. The following is an example of notes she wrote after a visit to a school in a long-stay hospital in West Yorkshire in 1975:

> Activities: staff piling up bricks.
>
> Lots of time on potting and feeding.
>
> No attempt to communicate with the children.
>
> Poor facilities – e.g. space, toilets.
>
> Insensitivity of staff and their lack of awareness: the school staff did not really know what they were doing.
>
> At least half of the children in the Special Care Class were not given any attention at all; staff had no special qualifications, saying 'we do not believe in them'. (OUA: 3/4)

It is interesting to note that these observations were recorded in 1975, well after the 1944 Education Act was repealed and the new Education Act, which had replaced it in 1971, had been hailed as bringing 'education to all'.

> On the ward:
>
> Abuse, minor but serious.
>
> Children remained on pots for up to two hours at a time.
>
> Out of the 24 children in the ward, there were 15 who never received any attention at all, not even a rude remark or a feel to see if they were dry. (OUA: 3/4)

During a visit to a long-stay hospital in East Anglia in 1975, her notes recorded that:

> Thomas, aged 12, received only 57 minutes attention in 10 hours.
>
> Rachel – becoming inquisitive and adventurous, i.e. 'a nuisance': recommendation was a harness-chair.
>
> Susan: attention paid to her in 10 hours 20 minutes was 1 hour 8 minutes. For 2 hours she sat in one position on a mattress in the school room.
>
> (OUA: 3/4)

Maureen also engaged in a dialogue with herself in her notes, analysing, questioning and trying to find reasons for the attitudes of the staff. Her notes built up a picture of neglect and abuse which Maureen was later able to use when she wrote her books. And throughout the notes her own voice is heard observing, suggesting, getting angry and being disgusted with what she saw. Again, this is a point we return to below.

Recording daily life: And noticing small acts of resistance

In her meticulous recording of everyday life, Maureen noted with care those few occasions when families, the League of Friends, women 'helpers', nurses or the children themselves spoke out or acted differently from expectations. Families who were critical because of their concern for their children, and who visited regularly, were often dismissed as 'fussy' (OUA: 1/2). They were a rarity. However, Maureen observed how the League of Friends in a hospital in the north-east of England, made up predominantly of parents, became the most 'militant' group, questioning day-to-day ward practices and 'demanding to take part in management' (OUA: 1/2). Collective action by parents was a more effective form of resistance than individual families speaking out, but was also a rarity. The women 'helpers' on the special care wards were themselves long-stay residents who came to help feed and look after the children – and who, through their caring role, were acting contrary to most people's expectations of them that were held at the time. For example, Maureen observed how 'Brenda' (all names are pseudonyms) formed a relationship with one of the children in the group she was assigned to: 'she did greatly care for Daphne, who had some ability, and gave Brenda some communication and affection' (OUA: 1/2).

There were relatively few acts of resistance on the part of nurses – but just occasionally Maureen observed and recorded those moments when one or more of the nurses defied the prevailing culture of non-involvement. The following example illustrates both the prevailing culture and the nurse's reaction against it:

> Valerie had lain in the same place and position for hours. Yet, she was an aware child. One of the qualified nurses explained how she sometimes 'coughed to get attention'. This nurse said they 'weren't supposed to cuddle the children because it spoilt them' but during lunch-time she *did* cuddle Valerie for ten minutes, saying 'a few minutes won't spoil you'. (OUA: 1/2)

The deprivation and loneliness experienced by the children often went unnoticed or at least unremarked by the nurses. There were, however, exceptions when nurses stepped back from their role and saw their charges as children with the same emotional and psychological needs as all children. Maureen recorded the following example in her field notes:

> One evening one of the older nursing auxiliaries, Mavis, who showed always a great deal of affection towards the children, cuddled Valerie as she fed her some Weetabix; and Mavis said how she wished all the children could be fostered 'by a loving person'. The nurses agreed, saying that they did not see the sense of 'programmes of play' as recommended by the Senior Nursing Officer but that what these children needed more than anything was loving, cuddling and mothering, and they [the staff] wished they could do more of this. (OUA: 1/2)

The children were rarely in a position to resist: 'They were the most deprived and excluded group of people within an isolated and deprived environment' (Oswin 2000, p.141). Nevertheless, there were occasions when the children did attempt to protest against their deprived lives: Maureen's field notes contain evidence of incidents of children swearing, pulling a chair over, opening and banging a cupboard door, and banging a clenched fist against a door. These were small incidents and were rare, perhaps because they had long proved to be either non-productive or counter-productive. Maureen observed Sally, for example, who she felt desperately needed a more structured day, opportunities for play and, most of all, 'a particular member of staff to care for her': 'But, nothing was being done for her, and the little attempts she was making to play and form elementary relationships with other children were not even noticed by the staff, let alone followed up' (OUA: 1/2).

Challenging the authorities through personal interventions

Maureen did not always remain quiet on her research visits; her research notes were only one way to change lives. There was always the more immediate, though more risky, method of engaging in dialogue with staff in each of the institutions. Building on her experience at St Mary's, over the next 20 years she challenged the authorities on-site, whether ward nurses, teachers, or social workers.

One example of this was her attempt to help a little girl, Rita, and her family. Rita was admitted to hospital when she was two years old because her mother was ill. When her mother recovered she wrote asking for permission to take her daughter home, but this was refused. Rita remained on the ward, the only one-to-one attention she received being the few minutes when she was force-fed Valium. In her research notes, Maureen wrote that she told the senior peripatetic teacher about Rita, hoping that action would be taken and, above all, hoping that she would be able to go home to her mother. On another occasion, she talked to the social worker and suggested ways in which another little girl could go home for Easter.

In the case of Rita, Maureen was protesting on behalf of families as well as children. Her notes show that she soon realized that parents too needed someone to champion their cause. She coined the phrase 'abandoned parents' (OUA: 3/4). She wrote about the 'lack of support by staff for families' and she was horrified by the remarks passed by staff about families who were trying to gain the return of their children. She noted down some of these comments, which, although this was 1975, sound as if they are being said in the early days of the 1913 Mental Deficiency Act, when families were visited, judged and kept under surveillance. Time had, it seems, stood still in these hospitals:

It's a dirty family.

They're all subnormal.

They have lice. (OUA: 3/4)

She discovered that the consultant often discouraged families from taking children home for good on the grounds of 'better for the child' and 'better for the family'. Maureen was resisting 60 years of bad practice and abuse (1913–1975), ingrained into the service whatever the legislation or policy changes.

Archives from many other institutions demonstrate how hard it was for parents to have their sons or daughters home once they had been admitted. There are letters from parents in the 1930s and 1940s requesting the return home of their offspring: many of these requests were turned down because judgements were made about the cleanliness of the home, or the fitness of the parents to have 'care and control' over their children (Rolph 2000, p.83). What Maureen discovered was that this was still common practice, even in the 1970s after the publication in 1971 of the influential White Paper *Better Services for the Mentally Handicapped*, which advocated more strongly than before for care in the community rather than in institutions.

On another occasion in a different hospital, there was another personal intervention by Maureen during her visit in 1975. On this occasion she took on the massed ranks of teachers, social workers, nurses and therapists, decrying the children's lack of attention. This time, unlike her experience at St Mary's, she felt she did not make any headway with the professionals: 'They looked pained and evasive, and made excuses about lack of resources, inflation, re-organisation of the NHS' (OUA: 3/4).

This particular hospital was regarded as a 'flagship', as being in 'the top league' of hospitals in Britain, and yet Maureen felt that, where children were concerned at least, criticism was justified. The severe deprivation she witnessed spurred her to try as before to argue for change. She talked to the social worker about the neglect, the lack of attention, lack of love, lack of any attempt to communicate with the children, but 'the deprivation was not recognised'. She did not give up, but, as she recorded in her notes, she 'met and had discussions with many different professionals, including social workers, voluntary societies'. She 'pinned down' the area nursing officer over the shortage of staff in the hospital, which Maureen felt was at the root of some of the neglect. She 'discussed plans for stepping-up voluntary work – a project for the weekends' (OUA: 3/4).

It is evident from her notes that Maureen not only interjected and remonstrated over individual cases, she also thought carefully about the issues and about the specific situation pertaining to each hospital. In addition, she offered suggestions for ways of alleviating the situation for both staff and children. Her interventions were not, therefore, simply angry outbursts or indignant condemnation of bad practice, but were attempts to be constructive and to offer solutions. She continued to hope that these interjections could have some immediate bearing on the lives of the children, as they had done in a small way in St Mary's.

Lack of resistance

In her field notes, Maureen cites evidence of this too-ready acceptance by everyone of poor environmental and material standards and poor professional practice. Why, for example, had Carl, aged 11, already waited nine months for a wheelchair that he 'desperately needs' and, without which, he spent his days lying on the floor staring at the ceiling? Most of all, why did no-one speak out on his behalf?

> It seems an awful indictment of lack of concern on the part of all staff – ward and school – that nobody sees it as their responsibility to speak up for Carl. Why do they so meekly let the situation continue? (OUA: 1/2)

Why were so many children in the special care wards excluded even from the on-site hospital school? And again, why did no-one speak up for them?

> Despite the Education Act stipulating that all children were to be included in educational services, the senior staff in the hospital fully accepted the exclusion of many children and the inability of the school to adapt its methods to suit the needs of these children. (OUA: 1/2)

Social workers also failed to speak out. Yet, as Maureen noted, they more than anyone were responsible for making sure that children living away from their families were well looked after – except, it seemed, when it came to the forgotten children in the special care wards. In her field notes, Maureen spoke out against their failure to speak or act on the children's behalf:

> It was amazing to think that social workers would not dream of placing children into a similarly run foster home or Children's Home, but placing them in ward like that was considered OK. Why are foster and Children's Homes judged on different criteria with regard to their suitability for long-term placement of handicapped children, than a hospital unit? Why don't social workers complain to their Directors of Social Services and say they do not like placing children into long-term unsuitable care? (OUA: 1/2)

Maureen was also critical in her turn of the nurses and teachers who had the day-to-day contact with and responsibility for the welfare of the children. She also saw, however, that there were some extenuating circumstances – that real barriers existed that prevented people from speaking out.

Barriers to resistance

Resistance was difficult, especially for the more 'hands on' nurses and teachers. It was not easy, as Maureen observed, for people in their position to challenge an entrenched regime (though at the same time she wished they would). The barriers to resistance included the built-in resistance to change of the regime itself – the environmental and structural factors that determined the nature of 'care' (and neglect). Other barriers followed from this: the position of nurses, particularly their lack of training and the stigma they experienced through their work; the misuse of power by individuals who were able to go unchallenged in such regimes; and the development over time of an uncaring culture. We explore each of these points in turn.

The regime: Environmental and structural factors

The children in the special care wards were living in long-stay hospitals which were far from being child-friendly:

> They are still run on traditional lines – unlike any other sort of substitute care. Patterns of care are dictated by the rules which are necessary for the efficient running of a large institution, not in order to meet the individual needs of growing children. (Oswin 1978, p.130)

The children, although in fact needing individual care, were put together in large groups within the institutions – becoming 'nothing more than compounds of distress' (Oswin 1971, p.134) The following extract from Maureen's diary account of a day on 'Snowdrop' ward indicates the poor quality of life for children there, particularly those excluded from school:

> Monday 16 June: The majority of Snowdrop children, 17 children (as 5 went to school, 2 went to the Play Sheds and 2 had a walk to the laundry) merely sat in the Caister chairs, or lay on the table, or in large prams in the courtyard, or sat in wheelchairs. This was from 9.30 until being fed at 11.30. (OUA: 1/2)

Although most of the 'special needs' children were excluded from school, some did attend, though often on a part-time basis. Attendance in itself was no panacea, however, and because of the nature of their disabilities the Snowdrop children were rather left to their own devices. An extract from Maureen's diary account indicated the unsuitability of the 'perfect freedom' (or neglect) model for the children:

> Class B, 26 June: The children didn't have a place of their own, where they could sit and get on with anything. They completely lacked any territorial structure. The idea of 'perfect freedom, so that things can happen' meant that the children's days were so unstructured that they merely milled about all the time, aimlessly. (OUA: 1/2)

The wards and schools were not, on the whole, run by totally uncaring people. The regime itself was inappropriate and this led to lack of continuity in care and consequently in relationships. Resistance in such conditions was difficult. Maureen summarized what she saw as the main barriers to good care:

- poor quality environment

- duty-orientated daily timetables (for example, in some hospitals children spent six hours a day in 'functional routines' such as toileting and bathing)

- changes of staff and fragmentation of care; not only did nurses change wards every three months, they were switched around every day within the ward

- the hospital hierarchy; hospitals were run by people not in contact with the children. This had encouraged an attitude of non-involvement and meant that 'poor child care practices are perpetuated from one generation of staff to another' (Oswin 1971, p.198).

The conditions in which teachers in hospital schools also worked meant that they as well as the children were isolated and unsupported. Maureen described a hospital school that she visited where three of the teachers worked all the time with children with high support needs (Oswin 1978, p.62). Each teacher worked in a separate room and the children came in small groups of three or four at a time for a morning or afternoon. She found they felt depressed about their work; they had little job satisfaction and felt lonely because they had little contact with either school or ward staff. They said they had little support in their work as the head teacher and their colleagues were more interested in the ambulant children. They also lacked practical support, for example, to take children on short journeys or to use the school's pottery and cookery facilities.

The position of nurses
LACK OF TRAINING

The years during which Maureen was observing and writing about the hospitals saw several important changes in government policy (1959 Act; 1971 White Paper). This period also saw the publication of several reports about the shocking conditions in long-stay hospitals such as Ely, Farleigh, South Ockendon and Normansfield. In the same era, Pauline Morris revealed more insights into the regimes in the mental handicap hospitals in her book *Put Away*, published in

1969. Despite this attention to abuses in hospitals, it may be that many of the nurses themselves were unaware of the crisis, and the moves towards new developments in learning disability. This lack of training and awareness – combined with both professional and geographical isolation – could have been one reason why nurses did not protest against the treatment of children. They had developed habits which did not change despite outside debates. According to Mitchell and Rafferty (2005), nurses on the whole seemed uninterested in the outside world – or were necessarily isolated from the outside world almost as much as the children themselves. One of the nurses interviewed by Mitchell said:

> Mental handicap trained nurses, I would say, generally weren't the best to educate themselves, weren't the best at looking at what was happening in relation to ministerial plans or whatever. If you asked nine out of ten of them what the Jay Report was, what 'Better Services' was, they couldn't give you three lines of it. They were not interested, never read journals, they never educated themselves or even bothered looking at reports, they left that to everybody else. I think a lot of the developments and plans and thinking was probably passing them by. (Mitchell and Rafferty 2005, p.83)

STIGMA

Maureen wrote about stigma in her notes. She referred to 'the sickness of a large institution – professional jealousy rife' (OUA: 3/4).

Maureen herself put forward some reasons for the behaviour of staff (OUA: 3/4). She built on the idea of stigma (Goffman 1961). She had noticed that staff were very uneasy whenever outsiders such as family or siblings visited the ward. It seemed that they already felt stigmatized by being mental handicap (learning disability) nurses, and felt threatened by the comparison between able children and their own 'charges', which was pointed up by any kind of mixing in the outside community – or bringing the community into the hospital. If they remained with the children within the hospital they would be 'protected', nobody would comment and nobody would draw any conclusions about them because of the children. Maureen wrote:

> To mix the children with more able children, take them out into the community, could be a painful and threatening experience for the staff. An example was a staff nurse at X Hospital who was so ashamed of being seen in public with his children who were so disabled. (OUA: 3/4)

This might explain the reluctance of the teachers, too, to allow Maureen to take the children into town. A lack of confidence about their jobs, career or role meant that they could not see beyond that, and therefore instead impoverished the children's lives.

Misuse of power

The long-stay hospitals were places where people could – at all levels – wield power over others without fear of challenge. This made resistance by relatively powerless people very difficult. Maureen noted several incidents of people misusing their positions:

> All the staff were quite rude to the children and really withering at times. On one occasion the staff nurse called Donna 'You hunchback, you!'

> It was very worrying to see that the Domestic, who was a very ignorant and bullying woman, had so much power over the children, and she was never corrected in her harsh behaviour towards them.

> The hospital school had a speech therapist but the head teacher refused to allow her on the wards, or even to advise the nurses. The head teacher was male, authoritarian and prone to anger. It was awful to realise that, through the head teacher's narrow-mindedness, the children who lived in the hospital would not receive speech therapy during the school holidays. And it was morally wrong that he should prevent her from visiting the wards at all or make contact with the nurses. (Extracts from OUA: 1/2)

An uncaring culture

In the course of her research, and in her later publications, Maureen identified a number of factors which had led to the uncaring culture that seemed to characterize the regimes she was studying. In particular, she noted:

- *Low aspirations on the part of nurses.* The total acceptance of the children's disabilities and the assumption that they had no other future than long-stay hospital care seemed to inhibit their aspirations for them.

- *Lack of initiative.* Staff suffered from 'hopeless defeat' – seeing disabilities as unchangeable, being unable to recognize any potential and being ignorant of other facilities.

- *Professional isolation:* The unchanging nature of the wards, the deprived environment and the attitudes of the longer-serving staff (which infected newer people with apathy).

- *Lack of understanding of child care:* This often manifested itself in lack of understanding of what the schools were doing and the importance of play.

- *Lack of support:* Staff suffered from 'professional depression' because they had no support, stimulation or guidance from anywhere outside the ward.

- *Habit of non-involvement:* This started from the duty hours and shift changes which made it difficult to build relationships – however, the regime discouraged closeness as it 'spoilt' the children.

- *Getting ahead of routines:* The widespread practice of preparing for the next disruptive event (laying night clothes out, preparing bath bundles and preparing for the arrival of the meals, for example) meant even less time was available for spending with the children.

Maureen's voice: The critical researcher

Throughout the field notes, and threaded through subsequent publications, is Maureen's voice as critic of the system and advocate for the children. She was first and foremost critical of a society that allowed such conditions to prevail and asked: 'have we really advanced very much in the last hundred years when we tolerate the existence of forgotten children – hidden children – only a few of whom have been described in this study?' (Oswin 1971, p.199).

Maureen was also critical of the system itself; the regime of the typical long-stay hospital which was inevitably at odds with the needs of children. She observed deprivation and poverty of experience on a day in, day out, never changing basis:

> It is a sobering thought that there are actually children in this country in 1970 who have never been into a café, never bought themselves an ice-cream, have never seen uncooked vegetables, fish and meat, or a loaf of bread. (Oswin 1971, p.204)

Maureen also observed the lack of continuity in caring and the absence of continuing relationships for the children:

> Because of the constantly changing staff and the work rotas in the big subnormality hospitals, a child may have one nurse get him up, another put him to bed, a third give him his lunch, yet another his tea, another may bath him and a strange face may see him when he cries in the night. (Oswin 1971, p.221)

In describing what she called 'Ward 7', Maureen critically drew attention to the shortcomings of all staff – at all levels:

> There were no therapists working in the hospital; social workers never visited the ward; the doctors gave no guidance at ward level, apparently because they were engrossed with committee work and with out-patients; the nurses appeared to be fighting a losing battle because of shortages of staff, and their good will and kindness were being dissipated by the poor conditions and lack of support. [...] The teachers said that they were aware of the poor child-care in the ward, but felt unable to do anything about it in case they spoilt the good relationship which existed between the school staff and the hospital staff. Their lack of action prompts the questions of how much will professionals shut their eyes to in the interests of preserving 'good relationships', and when do professional responsibilities towards the children have to take priority over good relationships? (Oswin 1978, pp.149–50)

The cost of resistance

Maureen paid a price for her resistance – for publicizing the plight of children with very severe disabilities. To her surprise, no-one welcomed the disclosures. Teaching colleagues were 'angry' with her for what they regarded as her 'disloyalty'. Nurses reacted more vociferously to the findings, sometimes taking a physical stance against her. Maureen later recalled 'the aggressive jostling by male nurses' on the occasions when she spoke in public about her research (Oswin 2000, p.144).

The findings were shocking and yet many doctors and nurses continued to deny that the children that Maureen had observed for hours, days and weeks were neglected both physically and emotionally. Doctors continued to insist that the children in the special care wards needed 'constant medical and nursing care' (Oswin 2000, p.144). Far from receiving constant care of any kind, Maureen's research had found that many children had as little as five minutes of personal attention in 12 hours of observation. As Maureen concluded: 'The children's lack of loving one-to-one care was one of the saddest aspects of their lives' (Oswin 2000, p.143).

'Resistance is a ceaseless, always unfinished task' (Said 2004). Even so, it's difficult to do – so what was it that made Maureen feel that she could resist, especially in the face of others' non-resistance?

1. She was an outsider

Although this may not have made it *easier* for her, it may at least have made it *possible*. It was certainly not easy because, although she was not at risk of losing her job like the nurses were, she still suffered for speaking out. She was treated to bullying and heckling at conferences; she was unpopular among the staff; she was never promoted; she had a poor pension. But did being an outsider make it possible to resist?

She was able to see things which the staff did not see. As an outsider she had not become institutionalized and she therefore was sensitive to the sights she observed on the wards. In some of the large former colonies, the nurses had been brought up as children themselves in families of nurses, living on-site in staff houses, and used to a culture of disparagement, name-calling and in-jokes (all of which Maureen noticed occurred on the wards of some hospitals). Maureen was outside this culture and was horrified and disgusted by what she saw and heard.

2. She was aware of research and developments in learning disability

Another reason for Maureen's ability to resist may also have been her knowledge of developments both in learning disability thinking and in the wider policy background. Unlike many of the nurses (Mitchell and Rafferty 2005) she followed the legislative developments and the hospital reports. She worked with Jack Tizard, who carried out ground-breaking research particularly in relation to children with learning difficulties. And she was a close friend of Peggy Jay who gave her enormous support at times in her life when she felt discouraged by her findings and their reception in some quarters (OUA). The Jay Report was published in 1979 and was influential in changing policies on nurse education. This background knowledge of the history of the institutions, as well as modern developments, we might suggest, gave Maureen an added awareness and a base from which to protest.

Conclusion

Maureen Oswin's work was multifaceted. She realized early on in her career that it would have to be this way, and that she would have to use many different methods to make any impression on the prejudice she uncovered. Simply challenging the rules as a teacher – although she did this on numerous occasions and often with considerable success – was not enough to change the system, which so often overpowered her good intentions. She told one story of how this became evident to her:

> The head teacher once appeared in my room and looked in horror at a child with severe learning difficulties in my group. 'But this child is severely subnormal' she cried out. The legal education wheels then turned and the child was transferred to the Foundation section of the hospital. Officials liked to sort out such muddles of administration and they soon weeded out any child who had slipped from the pigeon hole into which society had placed him. (Oswin 2000, p.138)

Undertaking long research projects had to run alongside Maureen's teaching work, therefore, in the battle for children's rights. Her notes and the resulting books had a profound effect on learning disability policy as regards children. She became the voice of the voiceless 12,000 children who lived in long-stay hospitals in the 1970s, resisting, as she said, the procedures of 'social services for not providing homes for handicapped healthy children, education authorities for not knowing what is going on and protesting about it, hospital staff for not critically looking at their child care practices' (OUA 3/4). Her published research began the process of enabling those conveniently 'pigeon-holed' to emerge from the hospitals to an ordinary life.

References

Goffman, E. (1961) *Asylums.* Harmondsworth: Penguin Books.

The Jay Report (1979) *Report of the Committee of Enquiry into Mental Handicap Nursing and Care.* Chairman: Peggy Jay. London: HMSO.

Korman, K. and Glennerster, H. (1990) *Hospital Closures.* Milton Keynes: Open University Press.

Mitchell, D. and Rafferty, A. (2005) '"I don't think they ever wanted to know about us": Oral history interviews with mental health nurses.' *Oral History,* spring, 77–87.

Morris, P. (1969) *Put Away: A Sociological Study of Institutions for the Mentally Retarded.* London: Routledge and Kegan Paul.

National Council for Civil Liberties (1951) *50,0000 Outside the Law.* London: NCCL.

Oswin, M. (1971) *The Empty Hours. A Study of the Weekend Life of Handicapped Children in Institutions.* Harmondsworth: Penguin Books.

Oswin, M. (1978) *Children Living in Long-stay Hospitals.* London: William Heinemann Medical Books.

Oswin, M. (2000) 'Revisiting the empty hours', in L. Brigham, D. Atkinson, M. Jackson, S. Rolph and J. Walmsley (eds) *Crossing Boundaries. Change and Continuity in the History of Learning Disability.* Kidderminster: BILD.

Rolph, S. (2000) 'Surprise journeys and border crossings', in L. Brigham, D. Atkinson, M. Jackson, S. Rolph and J. Walmsley (eds) *Crossing Boundaries. Change and Continuity in the History of Learning Disability.* Kidderminster: BILD.

Said, E. (2004) 'Terence Bowie, "The Last Jewish Intellectual".' *Al Ahram Weekly,* 712. Available at www.weekly.ahram.org.eg

16

Resistance and Control
Mutinies at Brentry

Peter Carpenter

Institutions for people with learning difficulties had lots of very different histories. Brentry, near Bristol, was started as an institution for people who had problems with drink. It slowly began to take people with learning difficulties as well. In 1901 many of the people who lived at Brentry rebelled against the staff and walked out of the institution. This sort of resistance carried on for many years and it was very difficult for staff to keep control. This shows that institutions were not always well ordered and that people resisted by rebelling against their conditions.

Introduction

The images of institutions for people with learning difficulties have included pictures of abuse and portrayals of residents as victims. Contrary images have been of people with learning difficulties as posing a danger to the rest of society and therefore in need of containment. This chapter helps to challenge this two-dimensional image by examining the early development of one institution, Brentry near Bristol, from the perspective of the resistance of people variously described as inmates, patients and residents to their compulsory detention. Records from the institution itself, as well as from local newspapers, provide a picture of a turbulent institution in which inmates frequently rebelled. The story of Brentry also gives an example of the way in which institutions took on a life of their own in that they were prepared to change their identity (or at least that of their residents) in order to survive.

The mutinous inebriate defectives

The group of people defined as 'mental defectives' by the Mental Deficiency Act of 1913 included a wide variety of people, some of whom were very resistant to their treatment. One such group was that of habitual drunkards or inebriates. There was a clear link between perceptions of inebriacy and mental deficiency. For example the 1899 Inebriacy Act had introduced a therapeutic experiment that included the involuntary incarceration of habitual drunkards by magistrates for a period of three years to reform their drinking habits. Most appeared to have reverted to drinking on return to the community and this was taken as evidence that they were mental defectives by the Royal Commission on the Care of the Feebleminded. Moreover, the link was emphasized by the fact that many institutions that were originally built for those described as 'inebriates' later became mental deficiency institutions.

The Brentry Inebriate Reformatory (known as the 'Royal Victoria Homes') in Bristol was the first and last such inebriate reformatory in the country and was one of the few that admitted men as well as women. It was initiated and managed by the Rev. Burden and his first wife, Kate. Although these places were seen by some to be therapeutic, they were like prisons as far as the inmates were concerned. The men regularly resisted and Brentry constantly ran into debt because of the large numbers of male staff that were required to keep the mutinous men in order. The records of the reformatory highlight several examples of the difficulty in maintaining order. For example the minutes of the reformatory meetings of 29 April 1901 record that:

> The majority of the male inmates are men who are only kept in their present state of control and discipline by the knowledge that there is always available sufficient physical force to restrain them. The documentary history of these men shows them to have been the most troublesome characters of the localities from which they have been sent... That as the cells have been almost continuously occupied by inmates who have been most subordinate and violent, it has been conclusively shown that the numbers of the police

have been no more than equal to the demand made upon them by the custody of these men.

Later that same year six inmates indulged in what the minutes described as an 'almost mutinous refusal to work, unless they received special remuneration for it' (minutes, 24 June 1901). The matter became so serious that the Home Office had to open a portion of Cardiff Prison as a State Inebriate Reformatory for the transfer of the ringleaders. A review of the minutes shows that abscondence and rebellious behaviour occurred periodically in the early years of the twentieth century and matters came to a head in the summer of 1909 when there was a mass walk-out that was sufficiently serious to be reported in the *Bristol Times and Mercury*. The following extracts are taken from articles published in the paper on the 5th and 6th of July 1909.

> Dr Fleck had warned the police to be in readiness, and last Saturday the matter came to a head. A complaint was made about the bread served for breakfast. It so happened that the thundery weather made the yeast 'go off' and that morning it was not so good as usual. Dr Fleck tested the bread, and told the men that it was not so nice as usual, but he and the other officers had used it. He also told them he had a fresh supply of yeast in, and they could have anything else, except bread. The men did not agree, but apparently marched down to the gate and got away…

> [After locking up the other inmates] as many attendants as could be spared set out after the recalcitrants, who had taken the road to Filton. The police were also informed, and Inspector Thompson, of Westbury, with one or two of his men, set off on their bicycles in pursuit. The alarm was also sent to all the surrounding village stations…and police were dispatched in vehicles and on bicycles in all directions. The fugitives, who were most of them in their shirt sleeves, as soon as they got outside the home armed themselves with tools, sticks and stones, and soon presented a very formidable appearance…so the police followed behind pushing their bicycles, carrying them where the ground was too rough to permit of riding or over stiles.

The upshot of the break-out was that the men were eventually persuaded to be locked up in the police station rather than be returned to the reformatory. The local magistrates court held a special sitting that imprisoned the ringleaders and later the medical superintendent was replaced by an ex-navy commander who, in the words of the reformatory's minutes, could instil the 'firm administration which an institution of this character must have' (minutes, 25 April 1910).

This group of people certainly resisted the conditions that they were placed in and their resistance helped lead eventually to the closure of Brentry as an inebriate reformatory. Like many other such institutions it changed from being an institution for those described as 'inebriates' to those described as 'mental defectives'. However, the change did not dramatically alter the pattern of resistance, as it appears that Brentry became a place for the detention of people who had become troublesome to other institutions and the combination of residents meant that trouble was inevitable. In 1921 an official visitor from Gloucestershire noted that 'it is stated to be practically impossible for the staff at Brentry to prevent absconding and the inhabitants in the neighbourhood of the institution have complained of offences committed by inmates of this class' (Gloucestershire Record Office CJ1/C2). Visitors frequently remarked on the problem of abscondence and the problem was such an issue for the superintendent that he sometimes felt that he needed to transfer inmates from Brentry. One such application from the superintendent to the board of control not only demonstrates the problem but also the very human side to the official story:

> Adjoining the Lower Village grounds there is a Market Garden where two young women are employed...they have attracted the attention of these two inmates and surreptitiously communications have passed between them. The inmates broke bounds during the evening of the 25 April and our Officers discovered them in a thickly covered wood two or three miles away in the company of the women. Owing to darkness they spent the night there and were rounded up in the early hours next morning and brought back to the Institution. I cautioned them and kept them in bed for three days to prevent a recurrance. This morning I intercepted [this] letter written...to one of the women...and the women will insist on walking along the public highway for the same purpose...

> My Darling Annie

> I am writing this few lines to you hoping you are quite well as it lave me. I have had 3 days bred and water and you can bet I am starving. Well dear I hope you have not done with me if you have I am going to run away again so for God sacke don't say you have. I hope you have not got in to any trubbul over me. I can not get enney sleep over you dear I hope you are not going out with that Frank I don't think you are dear because I trust you wile I am in hear and I want you to trust me do you think you could.

By the way did you send me enney fags up if you did I got them all write thank you. Well dear I think this is all for this time so good bye my God bless you and Jean always.

Frome your

Unhapey Boy Len

Write back to me as soon as you can.

Dear the Officers are going to send the rings back to you they wont let us have them.

(Gloucestershire Record Office CJ1/C2)

The problems experienced at Brentry demonstrate the extent to which people who were detained in institutions were prepared to go to resist their detention or to try to escape it. The institution was frequently criticized for its inability to control the people who lived there and the board of control put pressure on the management board to either sell Brentry or to improve it radically. An 'improvement' was finally made in the early 1930s when a new medical superintendent adopted a scheme of classifying the inmates and giving those who were classified as a higher grade responsibilities to discipline others. In return the 'higher grades' had freedoms and responsibilities not available to others. This was carried to the point of having a self-governing 'top grade' to be known for years to come as 'the grades'. This system seems to have been developed with the intricacy of a public school prefecture or an army non-commissioned officer cadre and was described as follows:

> The patients in these two blocks are allowed free parole on the estate. Each of the Blocks has selected a Committee of three. These three patients are responsible for the cleanliness of the Block, for the discipline and for the reports of cases of misbehaviour. As the patients are selected from the best behaved there is seldom any misbehaviour to be reported. Each Committee holds a meeting once a week and forwards the minutes to the Medical Superintendent. A member of the Staff visits once a day to issue articles from the stores and inspections are carried out at irregular hours… Up to the time of writing, the scheme has worked most satisfactorily. (de Mountjoie and Dudolf 1933, p.12)

Although the scheme appears to have had some success in 1933, by 1945 the then medical superintendent, Dr Mason, was again complaining of disciplinary problems. They were apparently compounded by some staff who, according to the medical superintendent, were at best lax and at worst in league with some of the criminal elements among the inmates.

> In practically every Colony at the present time, the high-grade new arrival receives almost unwarned the shock of propinquity with obvious mental abnormals. Complete segregation of other than idiots is usually impracticable. This shock is probably not much less than that likely in a normal person so situated. When mislead by false assurances immediately before arrival, the reaction is manifestly deepened...
>
> Parents and others frequently write unsuitable and inflammatory matter to the patient as well as to the medical superintendent. It is better to induce the writers by personal efforts to desist from this practice rather than exercise the power of suppression of such correspondence. In these cases it is nearly always intensely difficult to obtain the patient's real trust and co-operation, though the natural cunning of the defective often succeeds in an effective pretence of this.
>
> Such is the seamy side. My reason for stressing it is to support the plea that a Colony whose circumstances cause it to be populated with a higher proportion of delinquent defectives (whose natural bias is to be troublesome and hard to manage) should be staffed with reliable well-disciplined men in greater numbers proportionate to patients than that accepted in the general deficiency Colony. Some architectural protection against truancy is also necessary as we have found during the war years. Segregation of the hard cases, failures and debauchers in a special section so that their misdeeds do not disturb the Colony as a whole is probably also necessary. (Mason 1945, Bristol Record Office 40686/B/GF/1g)

This account shows that the institution remained difficult to manage until at least after the Second World War.

Conclusion

Whilst many texts refer to the success of the old mental defective colony, and it was portrayed publicly as a model of propriety and good care, in private it had to be acknowledged that the colonies only worked by means of a cooperation between staff and residents, which made it necessary for there to be rewards and privileges for cooperation by an inmate much as the current prison service works. This system has been endemic to the institution since involuntary incarceration was used, and can trace its roots to the systems of 'moral treatment' of the Georgian mad-houses.

This chapter has provided a picture of one institution that was clearly a problem to the authorities. Within its walls there were individuals with a wide range of abilities and many different perceived problems. These people resisted their forcible detention and ensured that their management was never easy for the authorities.

Reference

de Mountjoie, G. and Dudolf, A. (1933) *Brentry Colony: Medical and Administrative Reports 1933.* Bristol: Brentry Colony.

17

Taking a Stand Against the Odds

Kelley Johnson

Kelley Johnson has studied the lives of women who lived in locked wards in a hospital in Australia. Some of the women behaved in ways that have been described as challenging. Kelley asks whether this behaviour is resistance. It was mainly individual behaviour but it was the only way in which some of the women could get their own way. Resistance has to begin somewhere, and sometimes it has to begin with the individual.

Introduction

Usually when we think of resistance we think of groups of people taking a stand against oppression. Often such a stand is directed against policies or practices which are part of our public lives and which stop people from having good housing or employment or health services or sufficient income. But there are other forms of resistance to oppression sometimes taken by individuals alone and directed at the control of very private parts of their lives. This chapter explores how some women with learning disabilities have taken a stand alone to challenge systems that sought to manage their private worlds or their subjectivity. It draws on two pieces of research. Some years ago I worked with a group of women in a locked unit of a large institution who had been labelled as having learning disabilities and challenging behaviour. Their lives were closely watched and managed by staff but still individual women found ways to gain some control in their lives. The chapter will describe how they did this and how they were viewed by those around them. The second part of the chapter will describe the experiences of women who have experienced discrimination in forming relationships with others and how they have tried to resist the barriers which they encountered. The chapter finishes by exploring some of the factors which made the resistance of these women possible.

> We are in the society of the teacher-judge, the doctor judge, the educator-judge, the social worker judge, it is on them that the universal reign of the normative is based and each individual wherever he may find himself, subjects to it, his body, his gestures, his behaviour, his aptitudes, his achievements. (Foucault 1979, p.304)

Being in the kind of society described by this quotation means that our public behaviour is not only judged and managed through laws and social rules but our private behaviour also is subject to scrutiny, to judgement and then to practices which seek to shape and control it (Rose 1990). More than this in a society where the judges are everywhere, *who* we are as well as *what* we do is shaped and subject to the knowledge and the practices of professionals.

When people are judged as 'different' or 'other' because of particular attributed characteristics, for example learning disability, they become subject to knowledge and practices which focus on this perceived difference. For example, in the middle of the nineteenth century there was no clearly defined category of people with learning disabilities, no ways of measuring this 'characteristic' and no particular ways of thinking about people with learning disabilities as a group. Now there is a whole body of knowledge and practices which have developed about 'learning disability': IQ tests to define it, books and articles to describe and categorize various forms of it and sites where people who are labelled as having learning disabilities are 'placed' either to be managed or to be retrained (Fairclough 1992; Foucault 1979; Rose 1979).

When power is exercised so that it defines who we are and shapes our private lives it is very difficult to resist because there is no one organization, institution or group to whom we can direct our opposition (Fanon 1976). So for people with learning disabilities the knowledge and practices about their labelled difference is held by all of those with whom they come into contact whether or not they are sympathetic to the individual.

Self-advocacy organizations and groups have struggled effectively against the social effects of people being labelled as having a disability (Walmsley and

Dower 1997; Whittell *et al.* 1998) but the struggle to be defined differently as a person or to have the power to manage the very private parts of one's life is sometimes a lonely individual one.

The women in the locked unit

In the early 1990s I undertook a three-year study of the closure of a large institution for people with learning disabilities in Australia (Johnson 1998). For more than 20 months I was involved in ethnographic field work where I spent a great deal of time as a participant observer in a locked unit in the institution.

The 21 women who lived in the unit had been labelled as having learning disabilities and challenging behaviours. During the time I spent in the unit I talked with them, the staff who worked with them and their families or advocates. I was part of the everyday life of the women. I included in my research the ways decisions were made about the future lives of the women as the institution closed and they moved to either community living or to other institutions.

The women who lived in the unit were very different from each other in many ways. Their ages ranged from 26 to 72. Some had been in institutions since they were born, others had only come recently. Similarly some of the women had been in locked units for more than 20 years while others had only been there for six months. Eight of the women had no verbal language, six could speak to each other and to staff and the others used a small number of words creatively to make their needs known.

Within the unit there were nine locked doors and the women spent most of each day in one large day-room. Without staff permission women could not go from one room to another, have a drink or go to their bedroom.

The women spent the days sitting on lounges or chairs, pacing up and down, talking with staff, watching the television (when it was working) or attacking themselves, each other or, more rarely, the staff or the building itself. There was very little to do within the unit and the women rarely left it for any length of time.

Within the locked unit the women were under constant surveillance by the staff. For example staff decided when meals would be served and to whom, when the women would go to bed and get up, when they would bathe or shower and for how long, when they could leave the day-room and when they could watch television. The women had very little control over their lives. However, some of them did things which changed the way they lived. Let me give some examples (all names used in this chapter are pseudonyms).

Dora Craig and June Miles did not like each other. Yet for most of each day they were locked into the same room together. Sometimes they hit or bit each other in anger, sometimes they shouted at each other. They could not live separately because staff said there was nowhere else for them to go. But repeatedly, as I came into the unit first thing in the morning, I would find Dora excluded from the day-room and locked into the dining room. Staff would say that she and June had hit each other and should be separated for the day. If they were violent to each other early in the day they did not have to bear each other's company for hours. Their violence effectively ensured that their lives, for that day at least, would be less stressful.

Lena Johnson was aged 72. She had lived in the community all of her life until her mother went to live in a nursing home. She was now in the locked unit because some time after she came to the institution she began to hit some of the other women living with her in a more open unit. Although staff watched the women all day, and the bedrooms were locked, Lena would find her way into a closed or unsupervised part of the unit. Looking out of the window of the day-room, staff would see her climbing out of the windows and over the fence to leave the unit and the institution. She was always brought back. But she kept trying.

Brigid Anderson was a young woman of 26. She took her clothes off in the day-room sometimes 20 times a day. She would sit and wait as staff picked them up watching to see what they would do. Sometimes they would dress her. Often she would take her clothes off again immediately. Sometimes they would take the clothes away and pretend to hide them. She would chase the staff and shout loudly. Once I saw staff put her clothes on themselves. Brigid was furious.

The implications of the women's behaviour

Each time they occurred these women's activities changed the place in which they lived at least for a short time. Sometimes such actions changed where the women were located, sometimes they changed the way other people related to them and sometimes they changed their relationship with another woman living in the unit. For individual women there were short-term gains in the activity but there were also long-term costs which resulted in their continued detention in the locked unit.

The staff working with these women saw their activities as challenging behaviour. Such behaviour provided a confirmation to staff that the women needed to be in the locked unit and that they needed to be taught 'better' behaviour.

Women, sexuality and relationships

Most people expect to be able to form sexual relationships with other consenting adults and most believe that the choice about becoming a parent is a personal one. However, women with learning disabilities have often found it difficult to have close sexual relationships with others or to have children (Johnson *et al.* 2001; McCarthy 1999; Sigurjonsdóttir and Traustadóttir 2000; Slattery with Johnson 2000). However, some have resisted the control that others have exercised over this area of their lives.

Living Safer Sexual Lives was an action research study in which 25 people labelled as having learning disabilities told their life histories to researchers. Each person talked about their life to a researcher who taped the narrative. The narratives covered many different parts of the person's life but did have a focus on sexuality and relationships. The history was then written up from the transcript in the person's own words and taken back to them for discussion and for changes. The histories have been used to develop workshops for service providers, people with learning disabilities and families; to produce plain English booklets for people with learning disabilities; and to make videos (Frawley *et al.* 2003; Walmsley and Johnson 2003). This chapter draws on three of the narratives.

Molly Hope is a young woman who very much wants to have a child. She said:

> I want to have a baby at the moment and we're trying to get pregnant. I've been trying to get pregnant for 3 years and it hasn't worked… I accidentally fell pregnant once before to a friend. A one night stand I had. My mum and my dad and my sister didn't want me to have the baby, because I've got a disability and they reckoned I couldn't look after it. My sister booked me into having an abortion. And the day before, I had a miscarriage. Mum said to me 'Don't you ever do that again, because if you did you'd be disowned from this family'.
>
> I can't talk about stuff like that with my family 'cause they put me down all the time, and they just treat me like I've got a disability, and I can't do anything. I can talk to my boyfriend's mum about anything. She wants me to have a baby but my family don't 'cause they reckon I wouldn't be able to cope. (Frawley *et al.* 2003)

Molly's family wanted to prevent her from having a child. They succeeded the first time she became pregnant. She has since found someone else to support her.

Elaine Webster lived with her parents until her mother went to a nursing home. She then moved to a hostel. Her story provides an account of how her learning disability was perceived by those around her in relation to sexuality.

I've had a lot of boyfriends. James just wanted me to fuck with him. And I was very young at the time. Yeah I did have sex with him. It was good fun. He was nearly the same age as me. We got caught 'cause James used to come down and stay with us and James used to sneak into my room and we used to do it. And then my mother caught us and 'oh boy'. James said to me, 'Get back in your own bed. Your mother will be here.' James wanted me to go back to me own room. And James blamed me for getting caught with him. James said, 'You nut cake'. James wouldn't talk to me afterwards. And Mum was very angry. Dad came home from the pub. And oh boy. Did I cop it? Mum wouldn't let me see James again. Mum said I had to get me tubes tied. Mum said, 'It's up to you.' Mum said it was my life. She said, 'If you get your tubes tied you can have sex with any man you want to without getting pregnant.' I might have been, oh I was in my twenties when I had my tubes tied. And I said to Mum, 'Why can't I get married? I'm old enough.' Mum said, 'If you had a child it might turn out like you.' 'Cause Mum thought if I had a baby that might turn out with polio like me...

And then Mum said, 'What about having your tubes cut and tied?' Mum wanted me to have it done. The doctor said, 'You want to make your mum happy?' And I said, 'Yes. Of course I love me mother. 'Cause you've only got one mum.' And I said, 'Yes I want to make Mum happy.' 'Well what about it?' I didn't really have a choice. But there was nothing I could do about it. 'Cause I only had me tubes cut and tied to make me mum happy. (Frawley *et al.* 2003)

In spite of her mother's opposition Elaine had a number of different sexual relationships, some of which lasted a long time. However, in her 20 years of adulthood she had never had sex in her own home.

Hannah Booth and Kevin Ryan lived together in a special accommodation house.

Kevin is my boyfriend. He came here about six months ago and we fell in love. We wanted to share a room. The staff sometimes say things that we don't like. When they were saying it wasn't all right to share a room, we'd leave that particular night and go off on our own and then come back the next day. In the end they decided that we could have the room together.

It's fine living together. I have to tell his lizards to be quiet sometimes though. Kevin's easy to live with. He's really nice. I'm still asleep when he goes to work and he leaves me a letter every day before he goes to work. I buy him nice things. I'm on a pension but I like to get him something nice. Last week I got him a new wallet.

It's hard to get privacy. Sometimes we go into the city for the night but we can't afford to stay away for the night. We walk around and then we go to Pizza Hut in Russell Street. Some of the staff are friends of ours and we know the security guard very well. He lets us stay there. We talk to people.

Kevin's a really nice man, kind and we have a sexual relationship once a week on the weekends. Kevin's the type of guy that's not too hard, and agrees to have it once a week. On the weekends we go out and we're not here at the house, and that makes it easier. On a Saturday we go into the city and find somewhere else. We find a place where it's comfortable and OK to do it. There's a shop in the city where we find the privacy to do it. They've got a set of stairs that leads upstairs, and while they're busy, we sneak upstairs. (Frawley *et al.* 2003)

All of these accounts suggest that the women with learning disabilities were experiencing a high degree of control over a very private and intimate part of their lives and also over their desires and dreams. All of the accounts also suggest that each of these women found ways to resist such control: by finding other means of support than family, by finding ways to develop relationships hidden from those around them and by finding geographical spaces in which to have sex that were free from surveillance.

Discussion

These accounts of people's lives in different situations also share a common theme of control: either over their behaviour or their desires. For me they raise two important questions:

- Can the actions of individuals recorded in these accounts be called 'resistance'?
- What makes it possible for people to resist?

Are these actions resistance?

'Resistance' is a complex concept which is used very differently by theorists, researchers and activists. Some psychotherapists who work with individuals to change their internal worlds define it in terms of what the individual does to avoid changing themselves. The women's stories in both studies suggest that they were resisting imposed change from outside of themselves. Their actions seem to be an assertion of an internalized world of desires and thoughts.

However, a psychotherapeutic perspective is not the only one to resistance. More frequently it has been defined in terms of political action; for example: 'Actions that have some degree of consciousness and collectivity about them, as well as some explicit attention to broad structures of domination' (Rubin 1996, p.239).

At first it is difficult to know how far this definition is applicable to the accounts of the women's lives earlier in this chapter. It is not possible to know if the women in the locked unit were consciously resisting power or domination because they could not communicate verbally. Even when people can communicate verbally we do not always know if they are conscious of why they are doing what they are doing. Sometimes new strategies and actions emerge out of the success or failure of earlier ones. For example Molly's views about having children have not really changed but her strategies about how to succeed in doing this have altered as a result of her previous experience with her family.

The women could not change the attitudes or the power of those around them. Indeed, sometimes their actions of resistance confirmed these attitudes. For example, when women in the locked unit 'resisted' it was interpreted as challenging behaviour and confirmed for staff the need for them to be locked up. Yet these women persisted in their actions. They were trying to find spaces in the power around them where they could gain a little freedom and have some hope of achieving their desires or needs.

None of these women was taking collective action. That is they were not working together with a group to change the power that oppressed them. Rather they were alone in their struggles (except for Hannah and Kevin). However, some of them did seek allies to help them with their struggle; for example Molly, and Kevin and Hannah.

Because the women's actions were individual ones, Rubin would argue that they were not in fact resistance. It was what some writers would call 'accommodation' and 'negotiation' (Alonso 1992). Their efforts altered the power that oppressed them; sometimes it led to punishment and to pain for them.

It is important to be clear about how we use words like 'resistance'. If we use them too broadly then they lose their meaning and their power. If everything is resistance then what is its opposite?

However, I would want to argue that the stories I have told are testimonies of resistance. There are some issues in our lives where it is very difficult to take 'collective action'. For example, it is very difficult to share issues around sexuality with other people, although the gay and lesbian movement has sometimes done this very successfully. Often for individuals a struggle to express themselves sexually has to be a lonely struggle, as it was for the women with learning disabilities.

For the women in the locked unit there was no way of taking collective action. They had no contact with others outside the locked unit and were not able to talk about their experiences with each other. Of course, self-advocacy groups could have come in and taken action on the women's behalf. However, they did not. And yet in the end the women's actions have become collective. The stories of the women in the locked unit once they were heard formed part of the fight for the rights of other people in institutions which was begun by self-advocacy organizations in Victoria. The stories of people with learning disabilities about sexuality are now being used to challenge the views of those around them through workshops and publicity. Resistance may be slow in coming. And it has to begin somewhere and sometimes it has to begin with the individual.

What made it possible for these women to resist?

This is really an impossible question to answer. Yet there were some things which I think did lead to some of the women taking the actions they did.

Some of the women had an idea that alternative and less oppressive ways of life were possible for them. Kevin and Hannah believed that they should be able to live together and have sex together as two adults. Lena had lived for a long time in the community, she knew that there was a life outside the locked unit. When people are closed off from information and from the community they have less chance of knowing that alternatives exist.

Some women did get support from others. Molly found a way to 'go around' her parents' views about wanting a child. This was the beginning of fighting for what she wanted with other people who supported her.

Some women took action because the living situation in which they found themselves had become unbearable. This was particularly the case for the women in the locked unit. In this situation women took on different forms of resistance. Some responded directly in efforts to change the situation; others, like Elaine, hid their lives from those around them in order to achieve their desires.

Women learned that they could win. Sometimes individuals knew that if they took strong action people with the power would back away. So if Dora became very angry and upset, staff would seek to calm her down or give her what she wanted to avoid her violence. Even if the victories were small and did not change the overall world of the women, they were important in people taking action.

Conclusion

Testimonies of resistance are important. The publicizing of group or individual acts can lead others to feel stronger in taking on injustices in the society. Once we hear the individual account it is no longer a lone person acting, the action can become collective and more powerful.

References

Alonso, A. (1992) 'Work and gusto: Gender and recreation in a North Mexican Pueblo', in J. Calagione, D. Francis and D. Nugent (eds) *Workers' Expressions.* Albany: State University of New York Press.

Fairclough, N. (1992) *Discourse and Social Change.* Cambridge: Cambridge University Press.

Fanon, F. (1976) *The Wretched of the Earth.* London: Penguin.

Foucault, M. (1979) *Discipline and Punish. The Birth of the Prison.* London: Penguin.

Frawley, P., Johnson, K., Hillier, L. and Strong, R. (2003) *Living Safer Sexual Lives: A Training and Resource Pack for People with Learning Disabilities and Those Who Support Them.* Brighton: Pavilion.

Johnson, K. (1998) *Deinstitutionalising Women. An Ethnographic Study of Institutional Closure.* Melbourne: Cambridge University Press.

Johnson, K., Traustadóttir, R., Harrison, L., Hillier, L. and Sigurjonsdóttir, H.B. (2001) 'The possibility of choice: Women with intellectual disabilities talk about having children', in M. Priestley (ed.) *Disability and the Life Course.* Cambridge: Cambridge University Press.

McCarthy, M. (1999) *Sexuality and Women with Learning Disabilities.* London: Jessica Kingsley Publishers.

Rose, N. (1979) 'The psychological complex: mental measurement and social administration.' *Ideology and Consciousness,* 5, 5–68.

Rose, N. (1990) *Governing the Soul. The Shaping of the Private Self.* London: Routledge.

Rubin, J. (1996) 'Defining resistance: Contested interpretations of everyday acts.' *Studies in Law, Politics and Society,* 15, 237–60.

Sigurjonsdóttir, H.B. and Traustadóttir, R. (2000) 'Motherhood, family and community life', in R. Traustadóttir and K. Johnson (eds) *Women with Intellectual Disabilities. Finding a Place in the World.* London: Jessica Kingsley Publishers.

Slattery, J. with Johnson, K. (2000) 'Family, marriage, friends and work: This is my life', in R. Traustadóttir and K. Johnson (eds) *Women with Intellectual Disabilities. Finding a Place in the World.* London: Jessica Kingsley Publishers.

Walmsley, J. and Dower, J. (1997) 'Shouting the loudest: Self advocacy, power and diversity', in P. Ramcharan, G. Roberts, G. Grant and J. Borland (eds) *Empowerment in Everyday Life. Learning Disability.* London: Jessica Kingsley Publishers.

Walmsley, J. and Johnson, K. (2003) *Inclusive Research with People with Learning Disabilities: Past, Present and Futures.* London: Jessica Kingsley Publishers.

Whittell, B., Ramcharan, P. and members of People First Cardiff and the Vale (1998) 'Speaking up for ourselves and each other', in L. Ward (ed.) *Innovations in Advocacy and Empowerment.* Chorley: Lisieux Hall Whittle-le-Woods.

PART IV

Alternative Interpretations

Reflections on Resistance

18

Assistance and Resistance
Making Sense of Inter-war Caring Strategies

Pamela Dale

People with learning difficulties and their families have sometimes been seen as victims of government policies of the past. The records from the south-west of England show that people were not always victims but were sometimes able to take control of their own lives. However, sometimes the needs of families were seen to be more important than the needs of people with learning difficulties. Families sometimes did not understand the abilities of people with learning difficulties. These views, along with those of some of the officials, were the most difficult to resist and it is only in more recent years that people with learning difficulties have been able to successfully resist what other people say about them.

Campaigning for the Mental Deficiency Act

The provisions of the Mental Deficiency Acts governed the treatment of people with learning difficulties between 1914 and 1959. Historians who have examined both the campaign for and implementation of this legislation have been concerned

that it suggests an 'acceptance of eugenic ideas, an eagerness for state intervention, and an intolerance which fit uncomfortably with the prevailing view [of]
British society' (Thomson 1998, p.1). There is no doubt that the Acts severely
restricted the lives of people with learning disabilities and their families. In recent
years, however, more attention has been paid to the care as well as control
measures that they introduced. This has allowed some commentators to talk
about the new services being part of a wider growth of twentieth-century state
welfare. Within expanded, reconfigured and different models of service delivery
service users, or at least their carers, are seen to negotiate with providers of institutional and community care despite an obvious imbalance of power and resources.
This chapter uses evidence from the archives of the Royal Western Counties Institution at Starcross in Devon to examine the form that these negotiations might
have taken and the potential benefits accruing from them. The term 'Starcross'
will be used throughout.

The idea of negotiation within the authoritarian language of the Mental
Deficiency Acts has been explored by Mathew Thomson (1998). He underlines
the contradictions in official thinking that made for ambiguities in practice and a
determination to maintain public support for the Acts by avoiding controversy
wherever possible. This allowed some scope for individuals and families to make
demands on service providers, for either more or less care and control, but did not
permit a wider debate that challenged the negative assumptions about service
users that underpinned the working of the Mental Deficiency Acts. Political
opposition to the Mental Deficiency Acts was confused by the cross-class and
cross-gender alliances that supported them, and tended to have both a maverick
quality and limited impact. One of the few Members of Parliament who registered strong objections to the Mental Deficiency Acts was Josiah Wedgwood.
While Mark Jackson (2004) reveals the force of Wedgwood's arguments, Mathew
Thomson (1998) shows how his opponents in parliamentary debates in 1912–13
and 1927 were able to dismiss him as an eccentric who was out of touch with
policy and practice. Press coverage was spasmodic, was far from favourable to
service users and did not lead to a concerted campaign to improve the opportunities available to people with learning difficulties. The odd sensational story
tended to suggest that mental deficiency cases were definitely abnormal; endors-
ing the scientific and pseudo-scientific theories that had originally justified their
identification and increasingly led to calls for their institutional segregation if not
sterilization on eugenic grounds. This further served to encourage special
measures to deal with the care and control needs apparently revealed by the work
of self-proclaimed mental deficiency experts. Thomson (1998) points out it was

the coalescence of concerns about threats to, as well as danger from, individuals designated as mentally defective that prompted the campaign for institutional segregation.

In the early decades of the twentieth century it appears that there was widespread official, and indeed public, concern about the problem of mental deficiency. Thomson has persuasively argued that it was the myriad of social and economic problems that became associated with the issue that led to the acceptance of measures for the control of people diagnosed as mentally defective while at the same time they were being explicitly rejected for other groups, including habitual criminals and the long-term unemployed (Thomson 1998). The provisions of the Acts certainly tell us much more about the preoccupations of contemporary social theorists than they do about the needs or experiences of people with learning disabilities.

The case for institutional control

The Mental Deficiency Acts did not arise out of the optimistic belief in the educational potential of disabled children that had founded some specialist residential facilities, including Starcross, in the mid-nineteenth century. Instead there was a negative focus on children who failed to benefit from 'normal' education once compulsory schooling was introduced in 1870. There was also concern that changes in the labour market made it difficult for these children to find work and support themselves after leaving school. Campaigners painted a bleak picture of inappropriate survival strategies involving crime, prostitution and pauperism. In the last quarter of the nineteenth century there was increasing support for the idea that significant numbers of people confined in prisons, reformatories and the workhouse were actually suffering from a learning disability and would benefit from intensive treatment in asylums designed to meet their special needs. In part this was a reflection of a wider nineteenth-century belief in institutional care as a panacea for a range of social problems, but while many projects were rejected on grounds of limited cost-effectiveness the association of mental deficiency with eugenic arguments stimulated action.

Institutions were created for the long-term, if not permanent, care of various categories of 'defectives' and there was a deliberate attempt to extend the surveillance of the suspected 'defectives' into the community to bring even those at risk of falling into crime, prostitution or pauperism under control. The association of all these concerns with the social problem group, later the 'problem family', confirmed that the patient's family and wider, usually working-class, community was also under suspicion and subject to a variety of official interventions. These coalesced around measures to control male violence and criminality, juvenile delinquents of both sexes and female sexuality.

Mental deficiency campaigners thus had a very clear idea of the target population for the new institutions they intended to create. However, the First World War delayed the immediate implementation of the 1913 Act and into the inter-war period the local authorities and voluntary organizations providing services had quite different concerns that centred on meeting their own priorities for mental deficiency work and avoiding unnecessary expenditure in a time of economic depression. As service providers they also had to give more attention to the opinions of client groups than the original campaigners, whose own practices were often more liberal than their rhetoric suggested (Jackson 2000).

Opportunities for resistance

The fact that services were first created, in opposition to parsimonious local politicians, and then fulfilled functions at variance to the aims of the original campaigners can be regarded as testimony to the resistance of people who were meant to be subject to the legislation, not participants in the policy-making process. However, this analysis is misleading as service users only exerted influence at certain points in the patient careers of family members. Instead it was competing professional interests and resource constraints that did more to shape services, although at moments of crisis various interest groups appealed to the needs of individuals and families.

A particular problem with mental deficiency work was that the total number of people with learning disabilities was unknown, but was definitely greater than the number of institutional places available. This meant that admissions to institutions were more difficult, and discharges more common, than the campaigners had anticipated. This provided some scope for negotiation over who would be admitted, and when. While the clear intention behind the Mental Deficiency Acts was to prioritize the admission of cases variously defined as 'young', 'high-grade' and 'morally defective' with the aim of securing their long-term care, families tended to press for help with nursing individuals who were severely and multiply disabled (Thomson 1998).

Relatives also wanted a form of respite care to help overburdened carers and requested assistance with what might be called transition moments. Most families needed support when there were births or deaths in the family, periods of sickness or unemployment, retirement, children starting or leaving school, or a variety of other crisis moments. Relatives definitely regarded any arrangements made as temporary and expected to remain in contact with institutionalized family members. Yet their influence over the institutional care offered and received, as well as input into the discharge decision, depended on convincing the mental deficiency authorities that the family carers were respectable and responsible people who could be trusted to fulfil their care and control obligations. This meant that 'cooperative' families were rewarded with choices while non-cooperation/non-compliance was severely punished. This worked in different ways at different stages of the patient's career, although it should not be assumed that the interests of carers and cared for were identical.

From surveillance to advocacy

The working-class communities from which most of the patients were drawn were unable to completely avoid official surveillance. The few families who sought to evade this by 'flitting' between different local authority areas were both marginal in importance and subject to severely punitive measures when discovered as they were often re-labelled 'problem families' and had all their children, with and without learning difficulties, taken into care.

Since it was impossible to avoid scrutiny altogether, many families deliberately sought contact with the mental deficiency services as a way of securing financial help and practical assistance. This either delayed or completely prevented an official decision to seek institutional care. Some social workers preferred not to certify children in 'cooperative' families, allowing the family to retain more legal rights and discretion over future care decisions. The community care programme, designed to provide pre-admission surveillance, was modified to help families cope with day-to-day care tasks. The previously unknown needs of families, especially mothers who usually acted as the primary carers, were not only revealed but addressed through these contacts. Social workers first discovered the overburdened mother and then started to advocate on her behalf within previously male-dominated bureaucratic structures and institutional hierarchies. While help for the mother too often involved putting the child on a waiting list for institutional care, the relatives involved retained much more control over the process than families subject to compulsory powers.

In the inter-war period social workers working for the Devon and Plymouth Voluntary Associations were an important resource for families. They offered advice, practical help and somebody for parents to talk to about their needs and experiences. They assisted with issues as diverse as accommodation, equipment, finances, day care, education, work and medical care, which was not otherwise available before the advent of the National Health Service.

Some families were supported by these arrangements for many years. Despite sensational reports in contemporary sources as well as historical accounts there is no evidence to support the idea that the mental deficiency authorities in the Devon area wanted or were able to institutionalize all the cases that came to their attention. Where the person suffering from a learning disability was in good health and well looked after there was every reason to support home care. It was only when that person was in poor health, or the carers became too sick or aged to cope, that the authorities stepped in. A chronic shortage of beds meant that many families who believed they had exhausted their caring resources had to wait months, even years, for an institutional place to become available.

In these circumstances, some families felt neglected by the system and tried to secure more care. They didn't just want assistance with personal care tasks but were keen for their children to have access to high-quality special education and training facilities as well as opportunities for socializing and recreation. These programmes and resources were only available in institutions. Many families were disappointed to find that the only comprehensive care package available was a bed at a mental deficiency institution; however, with varying degrees of reluctance institutional care was accepted by many parents as the best option for their children. Only one girl was forcibly removed from her parents and here there was some evidence that she had been neglected and possibly abused at home (this was out of a total of 2503 admissions and re-admissions in the period 1914–39). Other parents were clearly loath to give up their children but succumbed to varying degrees of official pressure and also recognized the impracticality of ongoing home care. The decision to accept institutional care must be related to the practical difficulties of providing care at home during the years of slump and depression. Most of the families covered by the Starcross study struggled with unemployment, poverty, poor housing and chronic physical and mental health problems.

Parents who wanted a place for their child at Starcross sought and received support from doctors, teachers, social workers, friends, and family members. They wrote to the institution and discussed both ongoing problems with caring at home and the hope that a period of institutional care would improve the life chances of the person with a learning disability. This was a part of the institution's work that the staff were very keen to advertise. Parents were told about the wonderful facilities available at the institution, and cases where former patients had gone into secure employment were also used for publicity purposes. At this time conditions in the institution itself were improving as new accommodation was developed.

Choice within constraints

Large institutions can easily become remote from service users and their concerns, so while expanded and improved services delivered some benefits to patients and their families this was often incidental to other agendas. Starcross staff certainly worked in a context of providing long-term care and offered very limited scope for input from family carers. In the inter-war period it was social workers who bridged the gap between the institution and the family.

Once a child had been admitted to the institution, parents found it more diffi-cult to influence future decisions about their care. Starcross staff had a very pater-nalistic approach to the patients and believed that only they knew what was in the patients' best interests. The institution was also a very isolated institution that served a wide catchment area. Most parents found it difficult to visit the institu-tion and the staff often unfairly interpreted this as a lack of interest that justified ignoring written requests sent by relatives.

This situation was eased by the involvement of social workers who acted as family representatives. Here relations were cordial with staff treating individual and family requests and complaints, channelled through social workers, as legiti-mate and helpful. While the demands made on the institution were usually modest, asking for an adjustment to the care package rather than its termination, there is no doubt that patients moved around the hospital, between different institutions, and between institutional and community care in accordance with both their own wishes and at the request of their relatives.

Parents who gave the impression that they were supportive of institutional care were able to negotiate with the care providers. Where staff thought that the parents were genuinely concerned and had an ongoing relationship with the patient they went to a great deal of trouble to support family contact and meet parents' wishes. Patients were encouraged to have home visits, first for weekends and then regular holidays. Patients were also placed in work and offered periods of licence at the request of their relatives. The demonstrated ability of many former patients to support themselves in the community with the help of friends and relatives actually encouraged Starcross staff to think more creatively about community care schemes for patients who had no families. A variety of arrange-ments allowed large numbers of former patients to return to the community and have more independent and fulfilling lives in ways never intended by the Mental Deficiency Acts and their supporters.

Within and outside the institution, patients were encouraged to make decisions about their own care, although options tended to be limited. Patients were generally rewarded for good behaviour in the institution. This could take the form of parole, a more responsible job in the institution or transfer to one of the employment hostels where patients earned their own money and had considerable freedom to spend wages on material comforts and leisure activities. Patients who did well at the hostels were encouraged to take full-time work away from the institution and were eventually considered for discharge. Within the paternalistic model of care offered at Starcross it was these patients who were regarded as successes.

Self-determination and the possibility of discharge

This prescribed model of an orderly and carefully disciplined life for patients, and former patients, was explicitly rejected by some individuals and/or their families. They were determined to secure the right to what they perceived to be a 'normal life'. They wanted access to accommodation and employment as well as the right to marry and/or have children. In the context of the Mental Deficiency Acts these demands were extremely controversial and were strongly resisted throughout the inter-war period.

These concerns usually affected patients resident in institutions. Some broke out of the confines of Starcross in spectacular ways. Dramas where patients absconded and were then recaptured were a common occurrence. Frustrated patients made verbal and physical attacks on staff and fellow inmates: events that often led to sedation, seclusion and transfers to 'state institutions for dangerous defectives'. Relatives and friends involved in escapes risked criminal prosecution, with the worst punishments reserved for people who helped women get out of the institution in order to marry.

Patients tended to be more successful at exiting the institution through the official community care programme than a temporary escape. Documents from Starcross suggest that, where patients could find people outside of the institution to support their desire for independence, there were legitimate exits from institutional care. Here the role of family members, community figures and sympathetic employers were all crucial. Timing was all important as unexpected requests for discharge were met with hostility and official resistance and even officially sanctioned discharges were not without restrictions. Even people who only briefly attended the special school at Starcross were subject to a process of almost imme-diate recall to the institution throughout their lives. To be known as a 'mental defective' within the meaning of the Act could have terrible consequences for the future of any individual, regardless of ability and life skills. The language and def-initions of disability in this period are no longer regarded as acceptable and were certainly disempowering. At the time families struggled against negative labels but could do little to challenge prejudicial terminology. The debate about diag-nosis and definitions was left to lay and medical experts. Some teachers and social workers challenged prevailing ideas about disability but tended to focus on indi-vidual cases rather than the deficiencies of the system as a whole.

In this and other areas families had to work very hard to get their voices heard and any concessions made to them were on the basis that they had demonstrated their 'respectability' and 'suitability to care' by cooperating with the authorities. The policy framework created by the Mental Deficiency Acts showed little con-ception that parents retained rights and there was no understanding that people with learning difficulties were capable of making choices about their own futures. Yet work with service users challenged these perceptions. The problem was that success stories were seen as the result of individual circumstances and, rather than demonstrating the potential of people with learning disabilities, tended to rein-force the idea that close official scrutiny of the lives of service users was the only way of preventing inappropriate behaviours and inadequate care. To avoid institutionalization families had to provide evidence of continuing good behav-iour, and any lapse in standards led to long-term institutional care while the 'pa-tient' and carers were assessed for stability and the possibility of discharge. Yet, the shortage of accommodation and surveillance personnel meant much of what the families said had to be taken on trust and many of the cases that the authori-ties wished to pursue were neglected through lack of resources.

This led to a situation where some people with learning difficulties were exploited by the family members and/or employers who were meant to be safe-guarding their welfare. In some instances victims of this type of abuse were able to get social workers to advocate on their behalf. It was not uncommon for 'patients' receiving community care to move between jobs before they found one that suited them. Likewise, any community-based patient was automatically allowed to return to institutional care at his or her own request. In many such cases former patients clearly declared a preference for which institution, unit or ward they wanted to be admitted to and mentioned staff or patient friends that they wanted to be with. In the absence of meaningful alternatives, some patients found a degree of security and care within institutions and this should not be overlooked even though current practice confirms that this was very much a second-best experience.

Conclusion

The testimonies of resistance above fall into three main sections, which consider care before institutionalization, institutional care and the care offered to people licensed and discharged from institutions. Institutional records contain some very rich narratives of resistance and reveal how individuals and their families tried, and were sometimes able, to negotiate with service providers and access the care they wanted. Contacts between families and service providers raised awareness of the scale of unmet need and required the state, at a national and local level, to make more resources available. The grants and equipment made available to families were qualitatively different from the surveillance and control that the Mental Deficiency Acts were clearly intended to provide.

Families had to work within a system that ensured the main form of help available was institutional care, but it cannot be assumed that this was unacceptable to them. In fact carers often expressed strong support for institutional care, despite its obvious limitations for patients. Older carers who were worried about the welfare of their adult children after their death were especially likely to articulate this view but other parents certainly viewed temporary institutionalization as a realistic solution to short-term crises. These stays then extended if family circumstances remained problematic, the health or behaviour of the 'patient' failed to show the desired improvement or the process of institutionalization itself made it less likely that the individual and family could cope back at home. The family often became resigned to long-term care, even if this was not what they had initially envisaged, and in these circumstances acts of resistance by unwilling and unsupported patients were interpreted as evidence of disturbed behaviour that required longer and more intensive institutional treatment.

People with learning difficulties, and their families, have often been regarded simply as victims of punitive legislation and segregation policies. Many were, but evidence from the south-west of England suggests that people were able to shape their own care, despite the hostility and suspicion directed towards service users. Services that were designed to provide a network of control and surveillance could also be made to help, if families were able to get their needs recognized. Yet the negotiation between service user and service provider was often a vehicle for promoting the needs of carers at the expense of people with learning difficulties. Family members, as well as officials, tended to underestimate the abilities of people with learning disabilities and overlook their rights. It was these paternalistic attitudes that were most difficult to resist, perhaps explaining why it is only in recent years that people with learning disabilities have been able to challenge many of the assumptions made about them, make their own choices, and speak for themselves.

References

Jackson, M. (2000) *The Borderland of Imbecility: Medicine, Society and the Fabrication of the Feeble Mind in Late Victorian and Edwardian England.* Manchester: Manchester University Press.

Jackson, M. (2004) "'A Menace to the Good of Society": Class, fertility, and the feeble-minded in Edwardian England', in Jonathan Andrews and Anne Digby (eds) *Sex and Seclusion, Class and Custody: Perspectives on Gender and Class in the History of British and Irish Psychiatry.* The Wellcome Series in the History of Medicine, Clio Medica 73. Amersterdam: Rodopi.

Thomson, M. (1998) *The Problem of Mental Deficiency: Eugenics, Democracy and Social Policy in Britain c. 1870–1959.* Oxford: Clarendon Press.

19

Stereotyped Behaviour

Resistance by People with Profound Learning Difficulties

Melanie Nind

This chapter discusses whether the behaviour of some people with autism or profound learning difficulties can be seen as resistance. Although it is not an attempt to change the way we define behaviours, it is an attempt to get us to see behaviours in a much more complicated way. For example, it may be that someone who repeats lots of little actions has found the only way that they are able to control what is happening around them. Trying to change this behaviour may be taking away someone's power.

Introduction

'Stereotyped behaviour' is the term frequently used by professionals to describe behaviour by people with learning difficulties and autistic spectrum disorders that is repetitive, rhythmic, unvaried and high in frequency (Miller, Jones and Walsh 1996). This commonly takes the form of rocking, hand-flapping or twiddling string or fluff, but much more idiosyncratic movements may also be included. There is some overlap between stereotyped behaviour and behaviour that is self-injurious such as rhythmic eye-poking or face-slapping. Both stereotyped and self-injurious behaviour are largely regarded as harmful and undesirable. In this chapter I focus on the stereotyped behaviour of people with profound learning difficulties and discuss an alternative way of thinking about this.

There is a considerable literature on stereotyped behaviour, much of which sees the behaviour as lacking in purpose and in need of elimination or at least reduction. This literature is almost exclusively from the perspective of more powerful onlookers. One exception to this are accounts from people with autism who are able to relate what this stereotyped, ritualistic or self-stimulatory behaviour means to them. I write as a powerful onlooker, but also as someone who has spent a lot of time interacting with people with stereotyped behaviour, often through that behaviour. For some time now I have been exploring the idea that at least some stereotyped behaviour can be thought of as a kind of resistance. By this I mean a way in which people with severe or profound learning difficulties can gain some control over an environment that is ordinarily largely out of their control. This chapter is an exploration of whether it is helpful, or indeed plausible, to interpret stereotyped behaviour as a way of rejecting unwelcome demands and situations or a way of communicating non-compliance.

Stereotyped behaviour as resistance

Is it plausible?

In making the case that stereotyped behaviour is a form of resistance among people with profound learning difficulties a problem arises in relation to the issue of intentional communication. By definition, 'profound learning difficulties' means having communication abilities commensurate with an infant in the first year of life (Ware 1996). Most people at this stage are not just pre-verbal but pre-intentional, which brings into question being able to *intentionally* communicate resistance. However, if we adopt a model of communication that goes beyond the simplistic delivering of a pure message from sender to receiver and is instead about negotiating meaning (Grove *et al.* 1999) then possibilities open up. We know that much communication at the earliest levels relies on communication partners inferring intent. That is, communication requires the more able partner to use a certain amount of guesswork, using the context and their knowledge of the person, to interpret possible meaning in their behaviour. Moreover, it is by communication partners treating their behaviour as meaningful and communicative that the person with learning difficulties learns about their ability to communicate (Nind and Hewett 1994). Interpreting stereotyped behaviour as resistance does not necessarily mean that there was intention of such resistance, just that resistance is a possible interpretation we can work with. For the interpretation to be credible, of course, it should not contradict other more probable interpretations (Grove *et al.* 2000). Nonetheless, working to infer plausible meaning reflects a 'capacity' as opposed to 'deficit' approach, with the important attitudinal difference that supportive listening involves assuming competence rather than incompetence (Goodley 2000).

Is it helpful?

If interpreting stereotyped behaviour as resistance is plausible then is it useful? Evaluating this usefulness requires us to address the implications. People with profound learning difficulties are almost always seen as passive and helpless and one implication is that instead we see them as resistors. This is a more active role and contributes toward an image of more rounded human beings. Self-advocates have done much to challenge one-dimensional images of people with learning difficulties as perennially happy or perennially pitiful. Treating stereotyped behaviour as resistance enables us to include people with more profound learning difficulties as people who are complex and who seek power over their own lives. Equally important, treating stereotyped behaviour as resistance may help people with profound learning difficulties themselves to learn that they have options in communication.

In addressing matters of usefulness we must also ask what this would mean in terms of the responses of families, practitioners and advocates. Is there a danger that the person with profound learning difficulties will be seen as awkward and challenging? Will this bring with it notions of blame for 'bad' behaviour? Or will it mean that those interacting with the person with stereotyped behaviour ask questions of themselves about what is causing the behaviour and seek to amend the environment and their part in it so that need for the behaviour diminishes?

Looking back – where does history lead us?

Looking back at the history of responses to stereotyped behaviour can inform this discussion. We can look at the trends in the ways in which stereotyped behaviour has been interpreted and responded to. While recognizing that some viewpoints have transgressed boundaries of time there is a sense of some historical pattern. The dominant view of stereotyped behaviours has been that they are 'inappropriate'; they have been widely regarded as a barrier to both learning and social acceptance and even harmful. Accompanying this dominant view has been the vast attention given to developing and researching procedures to eliminate or reduce stereotyped behaviours.

The view of stereotyped behaviour as something to be reduced has been lasting, but the detail of how to respond to bring about the reduction has undergone considerable change. There has been a tangible shift of focus from aversive to non-aversive procedures. Thus, with a growing emphasis on people's human rights, it is no longer acceptable to use procedures such as taps to the hand, arm splints or electric shocks. It is more common for people to be diverted from their behaviour or for alternatives to be encouraged, though verbal reprimands and negative feeling toward the behaviour still abound.

Another trend has been that the rationale for reduction procedures has increasingly focused on the need to prepare individuals with learning difficulties and stereotyped behaviour for their involvement in mixed settings. With greater community presence professionals have felt the need to educate, train or modify individuals to help them gain acceptance from others. A concern with the well-being of the person with learning difficulties can be intermingled with feelings of discomfort, embarrassment, helplessness or even shame among staff (Neufeldt *et al.* 1998), whose image is also affected by what they do. These feelings may have been more influential than the needs, rights and wants of people with learning difficulties themselves (Nind and Kellett 2002). Nonetheless, the justification that stereotyped behaviour may lead to impoverished social relations with others (Duker *et al.* 1989) has been powerful. By reducing the behaviour, it is hoped that the negative consequences of the behaviour can also be reduced.

The view that reduction procedures for stereotyped behaviour are necessary for the good of the person with learning difficulties incorporates the view that the behaviour has no adaptive function (Baumeister 1978) – no purpose. Without this dismissal of what the behaviour might mean to the person such intervention would be more problematic. Dismissing the behaviour as meaningless in turn requires that the person engaged in the behaviour lacks power and other people with more power are able to make judgements (Foucault 1979). The drumming of fingers or repetitive doodling in a business meeting does not lead to calls for a reduction procedure to allow the professional to be accepted by others. Who does the behaviour is vital to the way it is construed and to the response from others (Murdoch 1997).

An alternative view identifiable in the (mostly more recent) literature is that stereotyped behaviour does have some function for the person. From this perspective stereotyped behaviour might simply be self-stimulatory – enhancing stimulation in the boredom associated with institutions, for example. Or it might be stimulus reducing, by shutting out other aspects of noisy or demanding environments (Miller *et al.* 1996). In more sophisticated models stereotyped behaviour might be seen as homeostatic (Nijhof, Joha and Pekelharing 1998) – helping individuals to achieve equilibrium in their sensory stimulation.

This view of stereotyped behaviour as functional reflects a greater willingness to see the world from the viewpoint of persons with learning difficulties themselves. Individuals are seen as exercising some basic choice by selecting self-stimulatory behaviour, and indeed selecting particular behaviours over others and engaging in them in particular contexts. According to this way of thinking stereotyped behaviour does not disappear because the reduction procedure has made it less rewarding or reinforcing, but because the behaviour ceases to satisfy the individual's needs. This implies a more active role for the person with learning difficulties.

Notions of stereotyped behaviour as functional for the person have brought with them different notions of appropriate intervention. An obvious example is the willingness to see stereotyped behaviour as having some communicative significance (see, for example, Carr and Durand 1985; Donnellan *et al.* 1984; Durand 1990) which is associated with intervening to teach more acceptable alternative ways of communicating.

There have also been developments in which the emphasis has shifted from responding to a person's stereotyped behaviour to responding to the person as a whole. In Intensive Interaction (Nind and Hewett 1994, 2001), for example, intervention is geared toward facilitating social and communication development in individuals with profound learning difficulties in ways that respond positively to the individuals and with this to their stereotyped behaviour. Here the behaviour is seen as an important part of the person's response to the world – whether this be shutting out, stimulating or just making the world more predictable and controllable. The behaviour is more likely to be seen as a possible point of connection, a place for joint action or mutual pleasure, than as in need of eradication (see Nind and Kellett 2002 for more detail).

In the trends outlined here we can see a pattern in which the person with learning difficulties becomes more central. However, none of the perspectives outlined have interpreted stereotyped behaviour as resistance as such. Other hypotheses have been too influential and worked against this. Ideas of stereotyped behaviour serving no function, or at the very least a basic stimulatory function, have dominated thinking. Equally dominant has been the idea that stereotyped behaviour is neuropathological in genesis; that is, that the behaviour begins from 'organic' factors within the child. Strong links are made with particular syndromes such as Rett's syndrome and Fragile X (Miller *et al.* 1996) and with particular impairments in the areas of ambulation, vision and autism.

Alternative ways of understanding stereotyped behaviour – resistance as an option

One challenge to the traditional problematization of stereotyped behaviour has come from highlighting its role in typical infant development as a necessary stage in cognitive development (for example, Murdoch 1997; Thelen 1979). Infants repeat activities and practise skills in order to produce a desired effect on their environment, and the similarities with stereotyped behaviour in older people with learning difficulties have been stressed.

Another challenge comes from the refusal to over-simplify the interactions or transactions involved with stereotyped behaviour. There has been a tendency to dwell on straightforward reinforcement patterns and not to consider the potential for professionals or carers to take responsibility for interpreting and responding in more complex ways. Miller *et al.*'s (1996) alternative 'interactive treatment model' breaks with this tradition by accepting that there is not enough evidence to support any one theory over another of why stereotyped behaviour begins and is maintained. Instead Miller *et al.* (p.9) assert that it is 'more useful to accept that a variety of different causes and maintaining variables are possible' and that it is 'important to consider the complex and interactive nature of stereotypy, which most models fail to consider'. Similarly, Guess and Carr (1991) combine organic, homeostatic and behavioural theories to describe a three-stage model in which stereotyped behaviour begins as an instinctive, involuntary response, then is used to maintain sensory equilibrium and ultimately is used to achieve particular outcomes.

In a complex model there is room for seeing resistance as having some part to play in our understanding of stereotyped behaviour. We also now have accounts of the perspectives of people with autism who engage in stereotyped behaviour to assist us with a kind of insider perspective. These various accounts endorse the notion of multiple drives at work: Donna Williams (1994, 1996) refers to a kind of discharge function when she discusses her stereotyped behaviour as linked with a release of tension or an expression of frustration in times of anxiety. Jared Blackburn, in contrast, acknowledges that 'I know that at least some of the things I do are self stimulatory' ('stimming') (discussed by Jones in Neufeldt *et al.* 1998, p.27). However, he offers some timely words of caution: 'I think people are trying to treat a diverse category of behaviours (i.e. "stereotypies") as a single monolithic entity, and thus failing to see differences in motivation or purpose' (from his website, cited by Neufeldt *et al.* 1998, p.27).

When people have more profound learning difficulties and are unable to explain their behaviour, however, we have to make informed guesses. Ephraim

(1989, p.12) describes some of the guesses he makes about the behaviour of a child who has difficulty understanding the world, based on an understanding of 'normal' patterns of development:

> In his search for success in making things happen he goes back to what he can do, which is wiggle his fingers and watch them. The feedback from his actions encourages him and he persists. After some time his fingers become a bit boring but whenever he moves to dealing with other things he starts failing and goes back to looking at his fingers. He will discover that he can make his fingers behave in new ways all of which are under his control. Over a long period he will develop a complex and subtle range of hand watching behaviours. Such a child may in the course of time begin to get quite good at dealing with objects but other things like people remain difficult and worrying…a good way of dealing with this is to fall back on situations which are under his control so he goes back to twiddling very expertly with objects such as twigs, pencils, cups or whatever.

The child described here is in some ways resisting engaging with that which is too complex for him – in small but important ways he is taking control. Ephraim (1989) explains how his thinking led him away from seeking to eliminate behaviours that he saw as a means of controlling the world and a source of security for the child. Instead this took him toward accepting and valuing the behaviours, joining in with the child as the basis for communicating about the child's choice of activity. Such thinking is becoming more influential. The Royal National Institute for the Blind (1993, p.14), for instance, caution:

> Staff need to think why they want someone to change, abandon or modify their [clients with multiple disabilities] behavior. They need to consider what they are doing and how, before they try to change another human being. What right have staff to make these demands? Have they anything better to offer?

An increasingly inclusive ethos leads us away from insisting on conformity and towards listening to unfamiliar voices and celebrating difference in dignified ways (Barton 1997). From this perspective we might seek approaches that enable people with profound learning difficulties to be able to choose between stereotyped behaviour and breaking out of such patterns to join others in interactions that have been made meaningful for them (Nind and Kellett 2002; Smith 1998). What is vital to such approaches and distinguishes them from reduction procedures is that resistance is not overpowered by more powerful others, but instead people with learning difficulties are supported in learning to interrupt their flow of behaviour for themselves (Samuel and Maggs 1998).

Implications

This chapter is not an argument for a simple and straightforward redefinition of stereotyped behaviour. Nor am I here making the case that stereotyped behaviour is without doubt a manifestation of resistance amongst people with profound learning difficulties. To adopt these positions would be to stretch a point too far. I am advocating, however, that people's behaviour, including stereotyped behaviour, is important. A person's day can be made up of a constant stream of stereotyped behaviours that are called upon in different intensities in different contexts. When people are under- or over-stimulated, when they are stressed or anxious, or when demands are made that are beyond their capability or understanding are all likely to be times when they engage in stereotyped behaviour. This is likely to be because this performs some function for the person including, perhaps, resistance.

I am also suggesting, as Corbett (1998) does, that playing with different interpretations and challenging dominant discourses is valid theoretical work with practical implications. If we accept that stereotyped behaviour serves some personal function then our responses to the person and their behaviour must reflect this. We have a history of dwelling on the negative impact of stereotyped behaviour ensuring that we attempt to deal with it. Even when the functions of the behaviour have been accepted the behaviour itself has still been seen as unacceptable and alternatives have been trained or conditioned. All these responses neglect to consider the issue of personal power. The personal power of a person with profound learning difficulties is likely to be severely limited, but is very much dependent on others creating interactions in which the consequences of behaviour can be seen (Harris 1994). The adoption of preferred behaviour is in some small way the exercising of personal power; choosing stereotyped behaviour may enable the person to have considerable impact on their day-to-day living. This might mean some power over light or noise levels, over textures or smells; it might mean the power to keep things very familiar, safe and predictable. If the very essence of resistance is the taking of power then people with profound learning difficulties can be seen as resistors.

The implications of this are complex. We may still want to see a person with profound learning difficulties move on from very limited repertoires of behaviour. But we should be wary of seeking to take personal power away from them. Instead we should seek to help extend their personal powers. This might be through developing their and our abilities to communicate and relate to one another. It might be through developing or encouraging alternatives that are meaningful for the person and equally within their control. It might be through ascribing social significance to stereotyped behaviour so that connections with social consequences can be seen and personal powers learned (Harris 1994). However we proceed, I suggest it should be in the spirit of doing things *with* people and not *to* them. And we should, I suggest, acknowledge that twiddling, rocking or eye-poking might just be one person's own testimony of resistance.

References

Barton, L. (1997) 'Inclusive education: Romantic, subversive or realistic?' *International Journal of Inclusive Education,* 1 (3), 231–42.

Baumeister, A.A. (1978) 'Origins and control of stereotyped movements', in C.E. Meyers (ed.) *Quality of Life in Severely and Profoundly Mentally Retarded People: Research Foundations for Improvement.* Washington DC: American Association in Mental Deficiency.

Carr, E. and Durand, V.M. (1985) 'Reducing behaviour problems through functional communication training.' *Journal of Applied Behaviour Analysis,* 18, 111–26.

Corbett, J. (1998) '"Voice" in emancipatory research: Imaginative listening', in P. Clough and L. Barton (eds) *Articulating with Difficulty: Research Voices in Inclusive Education.* London: Paul Chapman Publishing.

Donnellan, A.M., Mirenda, P.L., Mesraos, R.A. and Fassbender, L.L. (1984) 'Analyzing the communicative functions of aberrant behavior.' *Journal of the Association for Persons with Severe Handicaps,* 9, 201–12.

Duker, P.C., Boonekamp, J., ten Brummelhuis, Y., Hendrix, Y., Hermans, M., van Leeuwe, J. and Seys, D. (1989) 'Analysis of ward staff initiatives towards mentally retarded residents: Clues for intervention.' *Journal of Mental Deficiency Research,* 33, 55–7.

Durand, V.M. (1990) *Severe Behaviour Problems: A Functional Communication Training Approach.* New York: Guildford Press.

Ephraim, G. (1989) 'Idiosyncratic behaviour and how to encourage it!' *Talking Sense,* summer, 12–15.

Foucault, M. (1979) *Discipline and Punish: The Birth of the Prison.* London: Penguin.

Goodley, D. (2000) *Self-Advocacy in the Lives of People with Learning Difficulties.* Buckingham: Open University Press.

Grove, N. with Bunning, K., Porter, J. and Morgan, M. (2000) *See What I Mean: Guidelines to Aid Understanding of Communication by People with Severe and Profound Learning Disabilities.* Kidderminster: British Institute of Learning Difficulties.

Grove, N., Porter, J., Bunning, K. and Olsson, C. (1999) 'Interpreting the meaning of communication by people with severe and profound intellectual disabilities: Theoretical and methodological issues.' *Journal of Applied Research in Intellectual Disabilities,* 12, 190–208.

Guess, D. and Carr, E. (1991) 'Emergence and maintenance of stereotypy and self-injury.' *American Journal of Mental Retardation,* 96, 299–319.

Harris, J. (1994) 'Language, communication and personal power: A developmental perspective', in J. Coupe O'Kane and J. Goldbart (eds) *Taking Control: Enabling People with Learning Difficulties*. London: David Fulton.

Miller, B.Y., Jones, R.S.P. and Walsh, P.G. (1996) 'Towards an interactive treatment model of stereotyped behaviour.' *International Journal of Practical Approaches to Disability*, 20 (3), 9–16.

Murdoch, H. (1997) 'Stereotyped behaviours: How should we think about them?' *British Journal of Special Education*, 24 (2), 71–5.

Neufeldt, A.H., Bicklen, D., Feldman, M., Jones, R. and McDonald, S. (1998) 'Self-injurious and stereotypic behaviour: Commentary on the current state of knowledge.' *International Journal of Practical Approaches to Disability*, 22 (2/3), 26–31.

Nijhof, G., Joha, D. and Pekelharing, H. (1998) 'Aspects of stereotypic behaviour among autistic persons: A study of the literature.' *British Journal of Developmental Disabilities*, 44, 3–13.

Nind, M. and Hewett, D. (1994) *Access to Communication: Developing the Basics of Communication with People with Severe Learning Difficulties through Intensive Interaction*. London: David Fulton.

Nind, M. and Hewett, D. (2001) *A Practical Guide to Intensive Interaction*. Kidderminster: British Institute of Learning Disabilities.

Nind, M. and Kellett, M. (2002) 'Responding to individuals with severe learning difficulties and stereotyped behaviour: Challenges for an inclusive era.' *European Journal of Special Needs Education*, 17 (3), 265–82.

Royal National Institute for the Blind (1993) *Stereotypical Behaviour in People with Visual and Learning Disabilities. Focus Factsheet*. London: RNIB.

Samuel, J. and Maggs, J. (1998) 'Introducing Intensive Interaction for people with profound learning disabilities living in small staffed houses in the community', in D. Hewett and M. Nind (eds) *Interaction in Action: Reflections on the Use of Intensive Interaction*. London: David Fulton.

Smith, C. (1998) 'Jamie's story: Intensive Interaction in a college of further education', in D. Hewett and M. Nind (eds) *Interaction in Action: Reflections on the Use of Intensive Interaction*. London: David Fulton.

Thelen, E. (1979) 'Rhythmical stereotypies in normal human infants.' *Animal Behaviour*, 27, 699–715.

Ware, J. (1996) *Creating Responsive Environments for People with Profound and Multiple Learning Difficulties*. London: David Fulton.

Williams, D. (1994) *Somebody Somewhere*. New York: Times Books.

Williams, D. (1996) *Autism: An Inside-Out Approach*. London: Jessica Kingsley Publishers.

20

Conclusion

Duncan Mitchell

Before writing this conclusion I reread the chapters, then in their final draft, awaiting the last-minute editorial touches. Inevitably in a rereading I found fresh insights and occasionally had the sense of reading things for the first time. The overwhelming impression, however, was the richness and variety of experience within the accounts of resistance. In this final chapter I draw together some of the main themes and suggest ways in which this book can help in the understanding of learning disability and services that are designed for people with learning disabilities. I also want to tie in the theme of this book with some of the more recent work that has been undertaken in the social history of learning disability, which continues to provide a rich seam of material both for historical and contemporary social research. I undertook both tasks with a sense of trepidation because in the first place the themes in this book are many and varied and consequently difficult to summarize. Second, I find that the more that I hear about people's experience the more I realize that there is so much to learn about the whole concept of learning disability, especially in regard to its position as a social group. The relationship to other marginalized and oppressed groups requires further exploration, as does our understanding of social identity in relation to learning disability. It is also noteworthy that there are considerable similarities of experiences across different periods and different countries. The similarities underpin ideas about people with learning disabilities being not only a social group but also being part of a social movement to fight for equality with others. To some extent this has been reflected in the chapters of this book that, while mainly reflecting British experiences, also include work from Australia, Iceland, the United States and Canada.

One of the issues for accounts in this book has been the changing and sometimes difficult-to-define target of resistance. This book derives from a series of conferences about the social history of learning disability. When these conferences began there was a very heavy emphasis on stories of people who had survived lives lived in institutions built to contain people with learning disabilities. Institutional provision dominated services for many people with learning disabilities throughout the twentieth century and the theme of resistance to control within the institutions remains strong within the social history of learning disability. While this book certainly continues this theme with stories from a variety of institutions, it has also developed the story by discussing aspects of institutional resistance that have hitherto been neglected. In particular there has been an emphasis on people with profound learning difficulties that, once combined with the stories of people who are articulate enough to be able to tell their own stories, contributes to knowledge about different aspects of institutional life.

There is also now an increasing number of stories from people who have experience of life without the institutions. Some stories, such as those of Mabel Cooper and Gloria Ferris in Chapter 2, link their lives in an institution with their contribution to life once they left to live in the community. Others such as the advocacy groups are testament to both a widespread oppression that is experienced in the daily lives of many people with learning disabilities and also the organized way in which such oppression is now being resisted.

Part of the story of resistance is the struggle to lead ordinary lives; this struggle leads to extraordinary stories. Some, like Marjorie's in Chapter 4, are a lifelong campaign to control a personal life. Other stories relate a personal struggle with policies and processes such as the one associated with institutionalization and the system that removed Elizabeth's child in Chapter 3.

Some aspects of behaviour have been characterized in services as challenging or problematic. This book sees this in a different light as resistance. This then becomes a positive characteristic on behalf of people with learning disability and a challenge for services, rather than the problem for individuals that it is easily seen as being. This perspective on challenging behaviour is one that has been recognized informally within services for some time. Behaviours that are quite understandably seen as problematic by many staff can also be framed within the context of a struggle for control over individual surroundings. The accounts of such resistance within the chapters by Kelley Johnson (Chapter 17) and Melanie Nind (Chapter 19) explore such issues and help to provide an image of people who, rather than being passive recipients of care, are actively involved in shaping their environment.

Marjorie Chappell's story is initially of a mother who refused to accept the negative advice that she was given and fought against others, both professionals and members of her own family, to ensure that Marjorie had as good a start as possible. However, one of the most telling parts of Marjorie's story is that she eventually had to resist against her greatest ally to ensure her independence. Such a narrative is familiar to many who go through a phase of struggling for independence from their family. For Marjorie and her mother this was an unusually lengthy phase.

Exploring Experiences of Advocacy by People with Learning Disabilities has provided an outlet for people to discuss the ways in which they, and others, have fought against oppression. It has also enabled people to demonstrate the positive contribution that they have made to lives of others. Part of this has been through self-advocacy itself and the way that the movement has raised awareness of issues that affect people with learning disabilities and forced policy-makers to take note of people who have learning disabilities. It also includes stories such as those of Gloria Ferris who was for many years an unpaid carer within a large learning disability institution and Marjorie Chappell who contributed to her family's business for many years. This book has just touched the surface of such positive contributions that have also been explored in subsequent conferences within the social history of learning disability. A particular issue for people with learning disabilities is the extent to which their contributions have been properly rewarded and the theme of the 2003 conference 'Work, millstone or milestone?' helped to reflect this. It is evident from individual testimony that people with learning disabilities have played a significant part in society through their work (paid and unpaid) but that their contributions have often been overshadowed by alternative images such as helplessness and victim.

Jessa Chupik, in Chapter 12 on summer camps in Canada, examined the dilemma that people have about whether to support segregated or integrated services. The extent to which ideology is more or less important than pragmatic approaches to developing services is far from unknown to advocacy groups and also to many service providers. The theme of integration as opposed to segregated services is less explicit in other chapters but nevertheless provides a thread through many of them as people have tried to work through the various issues involved. Among these is the question of whether people with learning disabilities form an identifiable social group. The growth of the self-advocacy movement has certainly contributed to a growing self-identification of people with learning disabilities as a social group. Stories of resistance help to provide a history to social groups and this book has helped to provide such a background. The links that have been made in Chapter 8, on songs of resistance, suggest that songs of resistance from learning disability institutions need to be considered within a wider movement of folk and protest songs.

Such a movement has moved beyond its original stage, as Karen Spencer's story in Chapter 6 demonstrates. The difficulties that advocacy organizations face when they develop are explored in some detail in this chapter. Karen Spencer's own experience of being Chair of a federal People First organization includes examples of having to deal with difficult issues relating to staffing, disputes between individuals and complaints. However, although it is important to record these signs of growing maturity within the self-advocacy movement, it is also important not to overlook the work of the pioneers of self-advocacy. The work of such people as Ray Loomis and Tom Houlihan is celebrated in Paul Williams' chapter, Chapter 5, and the development of SUFA (Chapter 9), Carlisle (Chapter 10) and Huddersfield (Chapter 11) People First groups also explores this.

One of the remarkable features of the stories that people tell is the similarity of experiences of people with learning disabilities regardless of whether they have lived in institutions or not, and regardless of their country and surroundings. It is becoming more and more clear that stories of oppression, and resistance to oppression, are apparent in many countries, many periods and many different social circumstances.

This book has captured stories of resistance that were first collectively told at two conferences of the Social History of Learning Disability Research Group at the Open University. Since then there have been several more conferences and countless discussions about the experiences of people with learning disabilities. Individual accounts still include important tales of institutional life but are also increasingly discussing stories of life without large institutions. Many of these stories now include stories of organized resistance such as that of Karen Spencer, who are dealing with the complexities of running their own organizations. There are significant links between the past and the present. On the negative side this includes continuing tales of bullying, social isolation and difficulties in accessing services. On the positive side are stories of valued contributions to society, resilience and the ability of people with learning disabilities to live ordinary lives in the face of restrictions. The overarching story continues to be the one that is recorded in this book. There continues to be a significant tension between the needs that both people and systems have to control the lives of people with learning disabilities and the needs that people with learning disabilities have to resist such control in order to take full responsibility for their own lives. In providing an opportunity to testify to such resistance, the editors hope that this book helps further the independence of people with learning disabilities.

The Contributors

Dorothy Atkinson is Professor of Learning Disability in the Faculty of Health and Social Care at The Open University. Previously a social worker working with people with learning difficulties and their families, her OU post involves research and teaching on current and past policies and practice. Her current research interests include life history work with people with learning difficulties, their families and learning disability practitioners. She has co-edited a number of books on the history of learning disability, including *Forgotten Lives* (1997), *Crossing Boundaries* (2000) and *Witnesses to Change* (2005).

Heather Cadbury MSc PGC (Research Methods) BSc (Hons) SRN works as a freelance researcher and facilitator within the field of learning disability. Her research work in the past has included working with individuals with dementia, arthritis, and multiple sclerosis. Her work on the Normansfield Project involved collecting articles, letters, wage books and stories from individuals connected with life at this institution.

Peter Carpenter FRCPsych trained in Leicester in medicine and then psychiatry, where a professional involvement with genealogy and industrial archaeology became an interest in the history of psychiatry and the rescue of the records of the Leicester Asylums and history of Thomas Arnold. On moving to Bristol became interested in saving the records of the learning disability hospitals that were closing. He wrote on the history of the Bath institutions and on the Rev Burden and Brentry Inebriate Reformatory. He was recently chair of the Glenside Hospital Museum and is currently Consultant Psychiatrist in Learning Disability and Honorary Senior Clinical Lecturer Bristol University.

Dries Cautreels is Master in Educational Sciences (Orthopedagogics/Disability Studies) and Advisor at the Flemish self-advocacy group 'Our New Future', Belgium. His main interest is in the field of Human Rights in Disability Studies, narratives in research and services and the implementation of Disability Studies within services and daily practice. He now works as 'orthopedagoog' at DVC Sint-Jozef, an organization in Antwerp, Belgium, specialized in support services for people with profound learning and physical disabilities and multiple impairments.

Rohhss Chapman works in the area of inclusive research and partnership with people with learning difficulties in Cumbria. She works closely with the People First self-advocacy movement. Her PhD was about inclusion of people who receive services at all levels within organizations. Her current work includes an oral history project on the contributions and experiences of people with learning difficulties during the war years in Cumbria. She has written on inclusive research, partnership and self-advocacy, and is a co-editor of *Witnesses to Change* (2005).

Marjorie Chappell lives independently in Milton Keynes and spends her time working on her computer and speaking to various audiences about her experiences. During her life she has helped to run a business with her mother; made and marketed her own weaved rugs; and successfully struggled to live an independent life.

Jessa Chupik is a PhD candidate (ABD) in the Department of History and the History of Health and Medicine Unit at McMaster University, Ontario, Canada. She is a Hannah Scholar in the History of Medicine funded by Associated Medical Services. Jessa is also the student representative with the Disability History Association. Following the completion of her dissertation, she will begin a postdoctoral fellowship with the 'Hidden Costs/Invisible Contributions of "Dependent" Adults' project and will be based at Trent University (Ontario). In the past, she has worked for people with learning difficulties as a support worker and a recreation facilitator.

Mabel Cooper is a spokesperson on behalf of people with learning difficulties. Her background is in self-advocacy and for many years she was chairperson of Croydon and London People First groups. She has contributed to several books on the history of learning disability, including *Forgotten Lives* (1997), *Crossing Boundaries* (2000) and *Good Times, Bad Times* (2000). She is a regular speaker on television and radio and an occasional columnist for *Community Care*.

Pamela Dale is a Wellcome Fellow based in the Centre for Medical History at the University of Exeter and is currently working on a project exploring the relationship between health visitors and Medical Officers of Health. Her chapter draws on postgraduate research, supported by the Exeter University Foundation and the Arts and Humanities Research Board, which examined the implementation of the Mental Deficiency Acts.

Andy Docherty was a founder member of Carlisle People First. He is also co-chair of the National Forum. He has done a lot of work campaigning for people to take up Direct Payments; he has one himself and feels that it has changed his life. Andy lived in institutions for a large part of his life. He makes presentations about his experiences and is interested in Life History, and he has been working on his life story. He has travelled all over the world finding out and telling others about self-advocacy. His interests are Life History, institutions and Direct Payments.

Malcolm Eardley is the campaigns and publicity worker for Carlisle People First. He has spent many years working on anti-bullying and drawing attention to hate crime. He has written an autobiography, *The Way of Life: The Experiences of People with Learning Difficulties* (2000), published under Millennium Awards Scheme, Cumbria. Malcolm has travelled at home and abroad to present the work he has been involved in and is an active member of the Carlisle People First Research Team.

Gloria Ferris is a citizen advocate with many years' experience of advocacy. She works in a voluntary capacity with Advocacy Partners in Surrey, attending committee meetings and helping with staff appointments and training. She is a member of the Croydon Partnership Board. She has written her life story, and has used it as the basis of several presentations at conferences. She contributed to *Good Times, Bad Times* (2000).

Dan Goodley is Reader in Disability Studies at the University of Sheffield and co-director of the Research Centre of Applied Disability Studies. He is also an advisor to Huddersfield People First. His research focuses upon disability politics and theory, sociology and social policy, critical pedagogy, critical psychology and inclusive education. His main theoretical resources include poststructuralism, postmodernism and critical disability studies and he has adopted methodological approaches of ethnography, narrative and participatory research and his analytical resources include discourse analysis and narrative inquiry.

Elizabeth Harkness has been part of Carlisle People First since 2000. She had a post as manager of the Citizen Advocacy project across Cumbria. She is a member of the Research Team and has just finished a pilot project on self-advocacy and autism. Her interests are inclusive education and making information accessible to all. Elizabeth's post now is as an 'Advocacy in Day Services' project worker, making sure that people who use services have access to advocacy. She believes that people with learning difficulties should be able to study at universities and be able to do PhDs.

Jeremy Hoy has been a member of Huddersfield People First since it started in 1986. He enjoys travelling the world, his job at the Huddersfield Examiner newspaper and meeting new people.

Nigel Ingham has worked in adult education and the voluntary sector for the past 25 years and has developed inter-agency reminiscence and oral history projects in North West England and South East Scotland. Currently he is managing a Heritage Lottery Funded project archiving the residential and working culture of the Royal Albert Hospital, Lancaster, a former large Victorian long-stay institution for people with learning difficulties.

Kelley Johnson is a senior lecturer in social work at RMIT University in Melbourne Australia. She has worked with people with learning difficulties over the past 15 years as a researcher and as an advocate. She has worked with women with learning difficulties to support them in writing life histories, explored how to include people with learning difficulties in research that they see as useful and written about people leaving large institutions and moving into the community.

Sue Ledger has worked alongside people with learning difficulties in developing support services in the UK and with two overseas projects. She is currently managing a community service with an inner London authority and completing a PhD with The Open University on the subject of Life Stories from Inner London. Sue has a longstanding interest in learning difficulty research, has been a member of the Social History of Learning Disability Group at The Open University since 2001 and is particularly interested in models of inclusive research and the use of video and multi media technology in life story work.

Duncan Mitchell is Professor of Health and Disability at Manchester Metropolitan University and Head of Clinical Services at Manchester Learning Disability Partnership, the first holder of this joint appointment between the University and Partnership. Previously he was Head of the School of Nursing at the University of Salford. He has also worked as a Community Learning Disability Nurse and has lectured in learning disabilities, politics of health and history of nursing. Duncan is the author of papers on the history of learning disability, health and learning disability.

Melanie Nind is a Reader in Education at the University of Southampton, England. She has a keen interest in teaching approaches that enable people with learning difficulties (especially severe and profound difficulties) to be active learners. She has taught and researched in the area for ten years and worked directly teaching people with learning difficulties for ten years before that. She has published widely in this field and is known for her critique of approaches based on a narrow interpretation of normalization.

Katherine Owen has spent many years supporting people with learning difficulties in both their home and work environments, including working for two years at a day service in North London, and living for four years in the Lambeth L'Arche Community. Since then she has completed an MA in Disability Studies and worked for five years as a qualitative researcher at St George's Hospital Medical School. Here she carried out an ethnographic study of women with severe learning difficulties moving from a locked ward. She is currently doing a PhD at The Open University exploring people with learning difficulties' experiences of a day centre.

Sheena Rolph worked for 12 years in adult education for people with intellectual disabilities who were living in a large hospital outside Norwich, England. She then undertook oral history and archival research for her PhD thesis, 'The History of Community Care for People with Learning Difficulties in Norwich, 1930–1980: The Role of Two Hostels'. She is a research fellow at The Open University, continuing to work on her chosen field of the social history of community care for people with intellectual disabilities.

Paul Savage has been with 'Speaking Up For Action' (SUFA) for 10 years now. He works in the SUFA office, typing and sending letters to people and answering the telephone. When he first came to SUFA he did not know what advocacy was until he went to a launch party at Sheffield Mencap and asked someone from Sheffield Citizen Advocacy about joining this group. The group was thriving, with people with learning disabilities working to have their say about their rights, improve relations with professional people from Social Services, and raising public awareness. The services for people with learning disabilities are now improving all the time, true to the message from *Valuing People*, 'Nothing about us without us'.

Lindy Shufflebotham has worked for the past 25 years in both the statutory and voluntary sectors providing support to people with learning disabilities. Particular areas of interest include access to ordinary housing opportunities for all, user involvement in organisational strategy and governance arrangements and the role and contribution of voluntary and community sector organisations working outside service systems to enable better access to mainstream opportunities.

Karen Spencer is Chair of Central England People First. She lives with her two cats, Tyson and Tiggy, in Wellingborough. She won a national volunteer of the year award for innovations in 2005. She has received a specially minted medal for this.

Gudrún V. Stefánsdóttir is Assistant Professor at the Iceland University of Education and a doctoral student at the University of Iceland. Her thesis is based on life histories of people with intellectual disabilities born 1924–1950. She has worked with people with intellectual disabilities for many years as an advocate, care worker and lately as a researcher.

Elizabeth Tilley is completing her doctoral thesis at the Faculty of Health and Social Care, at The Open University. Her research explores the growth of different types of advocacy organizations for people with learning difficulties, using a combination of historical and social scientific methods. Her broader research interests are around the historic and contemporary roles of voluntarism in the field of learning disability, and the interface between voluntary groups and the state.

Louise Townson has been involved with Carlisle People First for the last 12 years. She is Project Director of the organization. In 2002 Louise became involved in the Government Taskforce, making sure that the *Valuing People* agenda was being followed within services. She became involved with the Carlisle People First Research Team on a number of projects which had strong links with The Open University. This has also led to her undertaking article reviews for *The British Journal of Learning Disabilities*. She has been involved in a number of publications through the Research Team. Her interest is in inclusive research.

Rannveig Traustadóttir is Professor in the Faculty of Social Science at the University of Iceland in Reykjavík. She has worked with people with disabilities as an advocate, direct-support worker, administrator, policy-maker and researcher since the late 1960s. Rannveig received her doctoral training at Syracuse University in the USA between 1986 and 1992. During that time she met Tom Allen and became involved in assisting him with writing his story. Rannveig has published widely in the area of disability. She has been active in Nordic disability research and is currently the president of NNDR, the Nordic Network on Disability Research.

Jan Walmsley is currently Assistant Director at the Health Foundation in London and is Visiting Professor in the History of Learning Disability at the Open University, UK. She has been interested in the history of learning disability since the mid-1980s, and has written extensively in this area. She is currently working on a history of community care for people with learning disabilities entitled *Care, Control and Citizenship* (2006).

Tina Wilkinson contributed to this book when she worked for 'Speaking Up For Action' (SUFA). She has had a variety of roles, including administration and accounts, supporting people with learning disabilities on a one-to-one basis, supporting group activities and co-ordinating big events, in particular the development of the Sheffield Learning Disability Parliament and more recently the Regional Parliament, the first of its kind in the UK.

Paul Williams is a lecturer in the School of Health and Social Care at the University of Reading. He teaches on anti-oppressive practice, on research, and on work with people with learning difficulties, mainly on social work courses. He was co-author of one of the first books on self-advocacy by people with learning difficulties, *We Can Speak For Ourselves* (1982).

Carl Worth has been a long-standing and popular member of 'Speaking Up For Action' (SUFA). He has been particularly involved in delivering the training that SUFA offer and has gained a lot of experience training professionals in the National Health Service, voluntary agencies and the local council. Carl also delivers presentations around the country about the work of SUFA and helps organize the Sheffield Learning Disability Parliament, or 'People's Parliament'. He enjoys sport, particularly ice hockey, in his spare time and is a long-time supporter of the Sheffield Steelers.

Subject Index

Author Index